To:

....

From:

....

Date:

....

RESTORATIVE DEVOTIONS

for Women

RESTORATIVE DEVOTIONS

for Women

180 Meditations for
Spiritual Healing and Refreshment

BARBOUR
PUBLISHING

Print ISBN 978-1-63609-996-5

Devotions written by: Terry Alburger, Emily Biggers, Darlene Franklin, Renae Green, Shanna Gregor, Linda Hang, Jennifer Vander Klipp, Tina Krause, Marian Leslie, Donna K. Maltese, Sabrina McDonald, Kelly McIntosh, Lydia Mindling, Betty Ost-Everley, MariLee Parrish, Iemema Ploscariu, Valorie Quesenberry, Carey Scott, Karin Dahl Silver, Janice Thompson, Stacey Thureen, Annie Tipton, Amy Trent.

Cover design: Greg Jackson, Thinkpen Design

Published by Barbour Publishing, Inc., 1810 Barbour Drive, Uhrichsville, Ohio 44683, www.barbourbooks.com

Our mission is to inspire the world with the life-changing message of the Bible.

Member of the
Evangelical Christian
Publishers Association

Printed in China.

Introduction

*Create in me a clean heart, O God; restore within me a sense
of being brand new. Do not throw me far away from Your
presence, and do not remove Your Holy Spirit from me.*
PSALM 51:10–11 VOICE

If your heart and soul need some refreshing today, then these 180
restorative devotions will inspire, uplift, and support.

Overflowing with relatable scripture selections, encouraging
devotions with faith-building takeaways, and heartfelt prayer
starters, *Restorative Devotions for Women* will help guide you on
the path to spiritual renewal and healing.

Be blessed!

Spirit of God

"Then my people will know that I am the Lord their God.
I sent them into captivity among the nations, and I brought
them back again to their land. I left none of them behind. I will
no longer hide my face from them, because I will pour out my
Spirit on the nation of Israel, declares the Almighty Lord."

EZEKIEL 39:28–29 GW

When you first put your trust in God, did you notice anything different? How about when you ask God for forgiveness and receive it; do you notice anything different?

Sin can hold us captive to the love, grace, and mercy of God that He wants us to fully experience. But when that wall comes down, God's spirit comes pouring out over you like the rushing waters of a river.

Proverbs 21:21 (GW) says: "Whoever pursues righteousness and mercy will find life, righteousness, and honor." As you pursue God, He'll fill you with more of Himself. As you trust God, you'll want to live in right standing with Him. He doesn't demand a perfect life from you, just one that is in relationship with Him. Ask Him for a new, fresh filling of His presence in your life today. Trust that He'll supply enough for you.

Abba Father, I want to turn away from my sins.
I ask for Your forgiveness and trust I will receive
it. Now, help me to forgive myself. And renew me
by filling me with more of Your Holy Spirit.

He Makes All Things New

Create in me a pure heart, O God, and renew a steadfast
spirit within me. Do not cast me from your presence or
take your Holy Spirit from me. Restore to me the joy of your
salvation and grant me a willing spirit, to sustain me.

PSALM 51:10–12 NIV

King David committed adultery and had the woman's husband killed in battle (see Psalm 51). Talk about guilt! Yet the Bible says David was a man after God's own heart. David truly loved God, and being a king with power, he messed up royally!

David had faith in God's goodness. He was truly repentant and expected to be restored to God's presence. He could not stand to be separated from God. He recognized that he must become clean again through the power of forgiveness.

Perhaps there have been times when you felt distant from God because of choices you made. There is no sin that is too big for God to cover or too small to bother Him with. He is willing to forgive, and He forgets when you ask Him. He expects you to do the same. If you don't let forgiven sin go, it can become a tool for torture for the enemy to use against you. God sent Jesus to the cross for you to restore you to relationship with Him.

Heavenly Father, thank You for sending Jesus to
pay for my sins. Forgive me and make me new.
Fill me with Your presence today. Amen.

Be Glad!

The Lord has done great things for us! We are glad!
PSALM 126:3 AMPC

Years of captivity, years of being unwilling residents in a foreign land, were suddenly over. The writer of Psalm 126 described the incredible event like this: "When the LORD brought back his exiles to Jerusalem, it was like a dream! We were filled with laughter, and we sang for joy. And the other nations said, 'What amazing things the LORD has done for them.' Yes, the LORD has done amazing things for us! What joy!" (vv. 1–3 NLT). But years of captivity meant everything wasn't perfection in Jerusalem. So the psalmist prayed for God to bring prosperity back just as He had brought the people back home, while anticipating the good times that spring out of the bad: "Restore our fortunes, LORD, as streams renew the desert. Those who plant in tears will harvest with shouts of joy. They weep as they go to plant their seed, but they sing as they return with the harvest" (vv. 4–6 NLT).

Are you running low on this kind of hope? By focusing on all God has done, you can learn to praise Him beforehand for things He is yet to do. Because the Lord *does* amazing things for you still today. What a reason to be glad!

Bring back good times, Lord. And until then, I am and will be glad because of the amazing things You do. Amen.

Unforsaken

*But the LORD is my fortress; my God is the mighty rock where
I hide. God will turn the sins of evil people back on them.*
PSALM 94:22–23 NLT

A lot has changed since the Psalms were written. But while modern society is different from the ancient world, a lot remains the same. Reading through the Psalms, we see that the people of biblical times were no strangers to just how wicked humankind could be. Evil people were doing evil things way back then too, and God's people called out to Him to make things right.

Yet even before God righted the wrongs, His people observed how He was still active in positive ways in their individual lives: "Joyful are those you discipline, LORD, those you teach with your instructions. You give them relief from troubled times until a pit is dug to capture the wicked" (Psalm 94:12–13 NLT). And again, "Unless the LORD had helped me, I would soon have settled in the silence of the grave. I cried out, 'I am slipping!' but your unfailing love, O LORD, supported me. When doubts filled my mind, your comfort gave me renewed hope and cheer" (Psalm 94:17–19 NLT). God *always* brings His goodness into the bad. Until that day when He abolishes all evil, we can look to Him, our fortress and rock of refuge.

God, sometimes it seems like wickedness is
everywhere. Help me find good things in You. Amen.

Approach God with Confidence

*Let us then approach God's throne of grace with
confidence, so that we may receive mercy and
find grace to help us in our time of need.*

HEBREWS 4:16 NIV

The dictionary defines *confidence* as the "faith or belief that one
will act in a right, proper, or effective way" or "the quality or state
of being certain." Both definitions fit the admonition written by
the author of Hebrews.

In this passage, Jesus' work on the cross and a description of
why He is our great high priest gives us the means to "approach
God's throne of grace with confidence." Jesus—100 percent God,
100 percent man—is the only one who fulfills God's demands for
holiness and righteousness in those who approach Him. When
we accept Christ's sacrifice on the cross, we believe that He paid
the blood ransom required to remove our sins from us, making
a relationship with God a reality. We do not have to adhere to a
set of dos and don'ts or jump through a lot of hoops that man
requires in order to gain an audience with our Father God. We
have confidence in Jesus Christ's ability to make us able to stand
before a holy God.

With that restored relationship, we are also certain that
when we approach God's throne in need of grace and mercy, we
will receive it. What a great and precious promise we can cling
to as we run the race set before us.

Father, thank You for the confidence that is ours because
of the work of Your Son, Jesus Christ, on the cross.

My Soul Thirsts for You!

As the deer pants for streams of water, so my soul pants for you, my God. My soul thirsts for God, for the living God. When can I go and meet with God?

PSALM 42:1–2 NIV

What a lovely image in Psalms, comparing a deer that pants for streams of water with the way one's soul thirsts for the Lord. For humans, we might experience a smoldering and sweaty day of yardwork, which ends in a terrible thirst. We can't wait to drink down that tall glass of lemonade or iced tea and be fully satisfied. How much more should we thirst for the company of our Lord? May it become our focus, our drive, and even our passion.

How do we love our God? Do we long to meet with Him? Do we look forward to those moments and call them precious? Do we savor them, learn from them, come away challenged, inspired, and refreshed by them? Then, do we long to tell others about our living God?

Dearest heavenly Father, I long for Your beautiful and pure and glorious presence, and I acknowledge that there is nothing on earth that will satisfy like You. My soul thirsts for You! Please be ever near me. In Jesus' name I pray, amen.

Transformed

Do not conform to the pattern of this world, but be transformed
by the renewing of your mind. Then you will be able to test and
approve what God's will is—his good, pleasing and perfect will.
ROMANS 12:2 NIV

Think back to your high school days. You likely did your best to
fit in, to be accepted. After all, it's normal human behavior to go
along with the crowd, especially in the teen years. The problem is
that peer pressure and fears of being excluded or bullied prompt
behavior that's perhaps not the best.

Today's scripture encourages believers to avoid conforming
to the pressures of the world and its myriad of temptations.
To steer away from the advertising world that urges you to buy
fashionable high-priced products; restaurants that encourage
you to eat far too much; the entertainment industry that offers
more violence and less quality in its productions.

In Peter's letter to the Romans, he states conformity is not
the answer. Instead, you are to turn your entire being over to God
and let His will and way re-create you.

Sister, do not conform to the ways of this world. Don't let this
society mold you into something you don't want to be. Rather, pray
to God and let Him transform you according to His almighty plan.

Dear Lord, help me to stay strong, to transform and
not conform, and to come to You with a new mindset.

From Personal Experience

And they shall know [from personal experience] that I am
the Lord their God, Who brought them forth out of the land of
Egypt that I might dwell among them; I am the Lord their God.

EXODUS 29:46 AMPC

We all have personal experiences that point to our Creator—times when we know God intervened. Take a moment to recall those moments when you knew He was the reason for your bravery, strength, wisdom, peace, or joy. Seasons you knew there was divine intervention on your behalf. Maybe you had the motivation to forgive someone you thought was unforgivable. Or you found the ability to love someone many considered unlovable. Maybe a broken marriage was fixed or an unexplained illness healed. Or maybe your heart was filled with confidence and courage at just the right moment. Chances are you have a storehouse full of personal experiences, courtesy of your heavenly Father.

It's important to remember God has a perfect track record in your life. You need to know He is real, alive, and active today. And it's vital that you can look back and recall those times He showed up, because it reminds you that if He's done it once, He will do it again. It's called hope.

Lord, thank You for the gift of personal experiences.
They are perfect reminders that You are working
in my life every day. And it's those memories that
help to encourage me to trust You even more.

The "Why?" Question

"Sir," Gideon replied, "if the LORD is with us, why has
all this happened to us? And where are all the miracles
our ancestors told us about? Didn't they say, 'The LORD
brought us up out of Egypt'? But now the LORD has
abandoned us and handed us over to the Midianites."

JUDGES 6:13 NLT

You've heard it hundreds of times: "If God really cared, then why did this happen?" "If He really loved me, why did that happen?"

The "why" question has plagued humankind all along. We've somehow convinced ourselves that God is cruel for not rescuing us from our hard times.

Yet life is hard. That's a fact. An indisputable one. Parents lose children. Loved ones pass away unexpectedly. Injustices occur. We can cry out to the heavens, "Why, Lord?" or we can continue to trust God even during the hardest seasons.

The truth is we won't have all the answers in this life. But there's a day coming when we will, and He can heal our broken hearts in the interim.

God, the only "why" question I feel compelled to ask today is "Why did You love me so much that You sent Your only Son to die for me?" I'm humbled and grateful for You and all You've done for me, Lord. Amen.

Strike to Heal

And the LORD will strike Egypt, striking and healing.
ISAIAH 19:22 ESV

It's one oracle of doom after another as Isaiah works his way through the nations God would judge. But don't lose track of God's heart in all that destruction, because God's aim is restoration.

Take Egypt. God reduced Egypt to a glimmer of its former glory, crushing its gods, its Nile, its princes. Yet God's striking is paired with healing. "GOD will wound Egypt, first hit and then heal." Why? So that "Egypt will come back to GOD, and GOD will listen to their prayers" (Isaiah 19:22 MSG).

Our Lord is a merciful God, and even now He is orchestrating events to achieve His ends, which are peace and blessing! God's Word promises harmony in the most conflict-ridden places. "There will be a highway from Egypt to Assyria," Isaiah says; "Assyria will go to Egypt, Egypt to Assyria" (Isaiah 19:23 HCSB), and the two nations will worship together. One day, God will bless equally people once split by enmity. Can you imagine? "Israel will take its place alongside Egypt and Assyria, sharing the blessing from the center. GOD-of-the-Angel-Armies, who blessed Israel, will generously bless them all: 'Blessed be Egypt, my people! . . . Blessed be Assyria, work of my hands! . . . Blessed be Israel, my heritage!' " (Isaiah 19:24–25 MSG).

Praise the God who strikes to heal.

You mend this broken world, Lord. Hallelujah!

The Power of God's Love

*Above all things have intense and unfailing love
for one another, for love covers a multitude of sins
[forgives and disregards the offenses of others].*

1 PETER 4:8 AMPC

Let's face it—we're human. As Christians, we endeavor to follow the teachings of Christ but fall short. Periodically our actions take the course of a runaway train. Maybe a brother tested your patience and your intolerance of his behavior ignited you to lash out in anger. Perhaps a sister in Christ took the credit publicly for some good work you did in private and you seethe. Or maybe someone falsely accused you and you retaliated.

Every believer is flawed, and too often we fail miserably. Peter—endowed with a few flaws of his own—admonished the church to love one another intensely. He, above all, had learned the power of repentance and forgiveness, having denied Christ three times after the Roman soldiers apprehended Jesus. Yet Peter was one of the first to see Jesus after His resurrection, and it was Peter who first reached Jesus on the Sea of Galilee. There, the Lord commissioned Peter to feed His sheep. After Jesus' ascension, Peter—the spokesman of the apostles—preached the sermon that resulted in the conversion of approximately three thousand souls (Acts 2:14–41).

Christ's love forgives and disregards the offenses of others. His love covers a multitude of sins. That's the power of God's love at work. Love resurrects, forgives, restores, and commissions us to reach others for the kingdom.

Jesus, teach me to love rather than to judge. Amen.

Rend Your Heart

"Even now," declares the LORD, "return to me with all your heart, with fasting and weeping and mourning." Rend your heart and not your garments. Return to the LORD your God, for he is gracious and compassionate, slow to anger and abounding in love, and he relents from sending calamity.
JOEL 2:12–13 NIV

One of the most dangerous things about religion is how easily one can pretend to be faithful. Jesus spoke to the religious leaders of His day, saying that they were beautiful goblets on the outside but on the inside they were dirty and broken. God's children need to have truly repentant hearts to avoid becoming spiritually dead on the inside. It does not matter if people put on a facade of holiness and of feeling sorry for their sins. If their hearts are not truly changed, then their lives will remain unchanged and far from God's blessings. Believers are told to break their hearts of sin so that God can fix them and make them work properly. When His children show remorse for the bad they committed, God is gracious to forgive and compassionate to heal and to restore. People can only begin to understand God's colossal love when they understand the depth and darkness of their own sin. Confess the brokenness and then rejoice in God's salvation.

Gracious Abba, reveal to Your children even
the most subconscious of wrongs, and let Your
daughters confess their sins knowing You are
the Father who forgives. Thank You for Your
great patience and Your abounding love.

The Blessed Watcher

*"Behold, I am coming as a thief. Blessed is
he who watches, and keeps his garments,
lest he walk naked and they see his shame."*

REVELATION 16:15 NKJV

Have you ever felt like your quiet time with God was just one of
many things on your to-do list? In the Garden of Gethsemane,
Jesus asked His disciples to watch and pray as He too prayed, just
hours before His betrayal. Instead, they fell asleep. (See Matthew
26:40–41; Mark 14:37–38.)

The way to overcome temptation is to keep watch and pray.
Watching means being alert and mindful of potential temptations,
sensitive to what God may be trying to point out to you, and being
spiritually prepared to fight. Temptation assaults where you are
most susceptible. On your own, you can't resist it; but watchful
prayer allows you to access God's power and defeat the enemy.

Just as you are to watch and pray to stay the threat of temptation, you are also called to watch and pray for Christ's return.
When you're watchful in prayer, you'll be alert and sensitive to
what God is doing in you and around you.

Ask God to point out things that make you vulnerable to the
enemy's schemes. Allow your time in prayer to prepare, refresh,
and renew you.

Lord, help me be the prayerful watcher
You've asked me to be. Help me listen and
obey You as I prepare for Your return.

Chin Up

*"Do not be afraid, Jacob my servant; do not be
dismayed, Israel. I will surely save you out of a
distant place, your descendants from the land
of their exile. Jacob will again have peace and
security, and no one will make him afraid."*

JEREMIAH 46:27 NIV

Peace. A part of many church services involves people wishing peace to those around them. "Peace be with you" is the phrase used by the clergy. The people's response is "And also with you." At this point, the congregants greet their fellow churchgoers with a handshake, a wave, or a hug to wish them peace.

In today's passage, God reassures the surviving Israelites that they will be safe. These exiles, now living in a strange place, away from their homeland, having lost everything, were certainly alone and afraid. But God was there to reassure them that He would restore peace and security once again.

God holds out that same promise to you today. He wants you to know that you are safe and sound in His hands. All you need to do to tap into that peace is to "let be and be still, and know (recognize and understand) that I am God. I will be exalted among the nations! I will be exalted in the earth!" (Psalm 46:10 AMPC).

Dear Lord, grant me Your peace, the peace You promised
Your people many years ago and that You continue to
promise to me today. Help me to trust in You always.

Daily Reminders

Brothers and sisters. . .encourage one another daily.
HEBREWS 3:12–13 NIV

Everyone needs reminders about their health. Doctors' offices hang posters to draw attention to healthy habits while patients wait for their appointments—how many minutes of exercise to do, how often to schedule checkups, the right vitamins to take. Though the Bible doesn't have posters, it does remind us how to stay spiritually healthy.

As hard as it is sometimes, sharing our lives with a community of believers is essential to our spiritual health. Hebrews 3 commands us to encourage each other daily, reminding each other of our hope in Christ. Otherwise, we may forget our Savior and turn away from Him in the face of life's difficulties, futilely looking for help elsewhere. Godly encouragement isn't just kind words; its proclamation of truth protects and restores hearts in danger of faltering.

Sometimes it's extremely hard to find the right words to reassure a hurting friend. We all probably recall a time when life was falling to pieces, and we weren't eager for a mini Bible lesson. However, be brave and trust the Spirit; speaking the truth to others as lovingly as we can is a holy duty, a labor of love (Ephesians 4:15). Finally, encouraging others protects us as well—when we share God's goodness and grace with another believer, we remind *ourselves* of the faithful Lord we love and trust.

Father God, let my mouth be filled with
encouraging words from You each day.

It's Okay to Be Sad

They mourned and wept and fasted till evening for Saul and his son Jonathan, and for the army of the LORD and for the nation of Israel, because they had fallen by the sword.
2 SAMUEL 1:12 NIV

Sometimes we think we must be brave when the storms of life hit. We put a smile on our face as if nothing is wrong. We see sadness as weakness, and we don't want that adjective to define us.

Yet life is rough, friend. We face heartache on a regular basis. Maybe it's working through divorce, death, or disease. It could be an unexpected betrayal or a child having to suffer the natural consequences of a bad decision. There are addictions, lawsuits, cross-country moves, and the loss of a job.

Life isn't fair or easy for anyone. Sorrow is something we all face. And it's okay to be sad. It's healthy to mourn. God gave you that powerful emotion to help you process upsetting situations. It's in those sad times He will help heal your heart.

But you can't live there. Life moves forward and so must you.

Embrace the sadness. Invite God into it. Ask for Him to heal your heart. And know that in time you will smile again.

Lord, it's hard for me to be honest about my sadness. I don't want to be a burden or seen as overly dramatic. Will You give me courage to feel those emotions and trust You for healing?

Let Him Be Your Everything

*My God, my Rock, in Him will I take refuge; my Shield
and the Horn of my salvation; my Stronghold and my
Refuge, my Savior—You save me from violence.*

2 SAMUEL 22:3 AMPC

What is God's role in your life? Take a moment and think of all the things He is to you. Say them out loud. Maybe jot them down on this page as a reminder when you need it. Because you will.

There is power in the spoken word. Many of us are audible learners, and so hearing the different ways God has blessed us is powerful. David knew that. As a matter of fact, he spoke today's verse (and full chapter) to the Lord. It was a form of worship, an acknowledgment, and a reminder.

So, friend, who is God to you? Like David, would you say He's your refuge and rock? Is He your stronghold, shield, and Savior? Maybe He's been your provider and physician, or friend and fortress? Is God your healer and hope? Is He your deliverer and delight?

Tell God your list, and thank Him for all the ways He's shown up for you and how He's impacted your life. Share your needs with God and ask for His help. Let Him be your everything.

Lord, thank You for being involved in my
life. I'm so grateful for who You are to me.
I see it now. My heart is so full!

Follow Jesus

*"On your way," said Jesus. "Your faith has saved
and healed you." In that very instant he recovered
his sight and followed Jesus down the road.*
MARK 10:52 MSG

Jesus spent time in Jericho and was leaving town with His disciples. On His way, a blind beggar named Bartimaeus cried out to Him. The beggar needed God's grace and mercy, for he was unable to see. So, Jesus called the man over and asked him what he wanted. Bartimaeus replied, "I want to see" (Mark 10:51 MSG). Jesus said, "On your way. . .your faith has saved and healed you." His sight restored, Bartimaeus "followed Jesus down the road" (Mark 10:52 MSG).

As you consider all the ways in which life can bring you down—for example, a health issue, loss of a job, loss of a friend or family member, seeing a child suffer—it may take a lot of effort to look up to God, to cry out for His unmerited favor and mercy, to throw off whatever may be hindering you, to run after the Lord, and to put your most ardent and heartfelt desire into words.

So, sister, today, even if it physically or emotionally hurts, pick your head up. Literally cry out to God for what you need most. Then, by faith, whether you receive an instant healing or complete silence, choose to follow Jesus.

Lord, in every season You, Your words,
Your touch. . .are all I need.

Aroma

For we are to God the pleasing aroma of Christ
among those who are being saved and those who are
perishing. To the one we are an aroma that brings
death; to the other, an aroma that brings life.

2 CORINTHIANS 2:15–16 NIV

Daily life is full of scents. You smell fresh breads baking or coffee brewing, roses blooming in garden pots, or popcorn popping at the movie theater. These are pleasant fragrances that bring up lovely thoughts and delightful feelings. And because you are saved in Christ, you yourself have a sweet smell to God. He delights to breathe you in.

For believers in Christ, it's refreshing and encouraging to be with other Christians. The abundance of everlasting life is fragrant. However, to those not saved by grace, the opposite can be true. You can expect there will be people who don't appreciate the hope, love, and faith that wafts around you. You are fragrant, but nonbelievers don't like your smell. For you are a reminder to them that God is ever present and that they are either denying His existence or standing in rebellion to His judgment.

Strive to not be offended by nonbelievers. Simply do what you are designed to do. Bloom with all the love and freedom of a child of God.

God, thank You for making me fragrant in
Christ—for making me represent abundant life.
Remind me that You always find delight in me.

Reflecting (on) Christ's Beauty

*And we all, who with unveiled faces contemplate the
Lord's glory, are being transformed into his image.*

2 CORINTHIANS 3:18 NIV

What are you thinking about? Careful. The act of contemplation
is powerful. Why else would teachers chide students when their
attention is anywhere but on the lesson? Their daydreams about
recess won't fuel their brains for mathematics. Contemplation
is a moral and transformative action too. Contemplating the
difficulties of a relationship could sway a person's commitment;
contemplating wealth (or the lack thereof) can create heart-
sinking envy. We pay attention to what we care about; what we
care about shapes and changes us.

Throughout scripture, Christians are called to fix their eyes
on Christ (Hebrews 12:1–2). Here in 2 Corinthians, Paul writes
about contemplating Jesus' glory—the Greek word translated
into English as "contemplate" means both "to meditate upon"
and "to reflect." Dwelling on Christ's life *transforms us* into being
more like Him.

Thinking on Jesus means to meditate on the truth we believe
about Him. The Word shows us a Savior who gave up His holy,
perfect life to restore the undeserving to Himself, who rose again
victorious over death! The Holy Spirit enables us to reflect Jesus'
loving, sacrificial character in "ever-increasing" measure as we
know and love Him better.

Father God, when my mind wanders, teach me to turn
my attention again to Christ and His beauty. Amen.

God, the Miracle Worker

Then Elisha went to the spring of the waters and cast
the salt in it and said, Thus says the Lord: I [not the salt]
have healed these waters; there shall not be any more
death, miscarriage or barrenness [and bereavement]
because of it. So the waters were healed to this day.

2 KINGS 2:21–22 AMPC

When a miracle occurs in your life, to whom do you give the credit? The miracle worker or God?

In today's reading, the men of Jericho said to the prophet Elisha, "You can see for yourself, master, how well our city is located. But the water is polluted and nothing grows" (2 Kings 2:19 MSG). Even animals were miscarrying and becoming barren. So, Elisha told the men of the city to bring him a bowl with some salt in it. He then cast some of the salt into the spring and proclaimed God's Word, telling them it was not the salt or Elisha that had healed the water but God Himself!

Today, as you look at the miracles in your life and beyond, seek to understand that it is God who is behind all the great works. He is the source of all creation, healing, and wonders on heaven and earth.

As I look around me, Lord, I see Your hand, Your love,
Your healing in it all. Thank You, Lord of wonder,
for all things. In Jesus' name I pray, amen.

God's Temple

*Don't you know that your body is a temple that belongs to the
Holy Spirit? The Holy Spirit, whom you received from God,
lives in you. You don't belong to yourselves. You were bought for
a price. So bring glory to God in the way you use your body.*

1 CORINTHIANS 6:19–20 GW

It's easy to compartmentalize faith. One wonders if the physical
body matters all that much since the new life in Christ is spiritual, a change of heart—and flesh and bones are a shell, a vestige
of the former way of life. One day they will be exchanged for an
imperishable, spiritual body (see 1 Corinthians 15:53).

Yet the call to be joined to Christ begins now, in the earthly
realm, with a believer's body as God's temple. Thus, when the
physical body is abused, God's temple is tarnished.

Imagine Jesus coming to dinner. How might you change the
externals? Would you try to hide unhealthy habits? Would you
dress differently or serve a different menu? What entertainment
would you plan?

God wants you to live every day with the knowledge—inside
and out—that He's a permanent resident in the heart, mind,
body, and soul of the believer. Treating your body with respect
is important because God lives there.

Indwelling Spirit, make repairs to my soul and
spirit that only You can so that I may glorify
You in my body and find the strength to take
the necessary steps to change. Amen.

A Promise of Great Things

"Why then did you bring me out of the womb? I wish I had died before any eye saw me. If only I had never come into being, or had been carried straight from the womb to the grave! Are not my few days almost over? Turn away from me so I can have a moment's joy before I go to the place of no return, to the land of gloom and utter darkness, to the land of deepest night, of utter darkness and disorder, where even the light is like darkness."

JOB 10:18–22 NIV

When we walk through the darkest valley, God is there. And even if we don't receive the help, the healing, the complete victory on this side of eternity, we will on the other side. As followers of Christ, we have promises of much more to come, promises that no mere man or woman on earth can make. Only Jesus says, "And if I go and prepare a place for you, I will come back and take you to be with me that you also may be where I am" (John 14:3 NIV).

When all is lost, and even when the light here has become like darkness, Christ comes with truth, assurances, and hope.

Know. Cling. Celebrate!

Lord, thank You for the beautiful
promise of heaven. Amen.

Hearts Greatly Moved

*And they said to one another, Were not our hearts
greatly moved and burning within us while He was
talking with us on the road and as He opened and
explained to us [the sense of] the Scriptures?*

LUKE 24:32 AMPC

Sometimes it can be difficult to understand what God is trying
to tell you in His Word. That's why there's such a great market for
different translations and study editions of Bibles. Yet even then,
it can still be difficult to fathom what God is saying. But when
you do, when a passage you've read at least fifty times suddenly
becomes clear, it's amazing how your heart is moved!

That's what two disciples walking to Emmaus experienced after Jesus' death and resurrection. They were talking about what'd
happened when they were joined by a stranger. Unbeknownst to
them, that stranger was Jesus! He began explaining to them how
all the recent events had been foretold in the scriptures. Then,
when they invited Him in for a meal and He blessed then broke
the bread, they realized the stranger was Jesus—and He vanished!

That same Jesus who walked with those two disciples on
their way to Emmaus is walking with you right now. And He's
ready to reveal Himself in the scriptures so you too can understand who He is. So, woman, open your Bible and pray for Jesus
to open your eyes.

Show me, Jesus, what You would have me
know and understand in this moment.

Cleansed and Rejuvenated

These are the instructions for the Whole-Burnt-
Offering, the Grain-Offering, the Absolution-Offering, the
Compensation-Offering, the Ordination-Offering, and the
Peace-Offering which GOD gave Moses at Mount Sinai
on the day he commanded the People of Israel to present
their offerings to GOD in the wilderness of Sinai.

LEVITICUS 7:37–38 MSG

God spoke to Moses so clearly, giving him very specific instructions on how each offering was to be conducted. A cleansing process that would hopefully provide peace and security for a person on the inside—mentally, emotionally, and spiritually—and on the outside, physically.

When you have made a mistake and know you need to apologize or ask for forgiveness, have you ever felt unclean figuratively? If so, imagine what it would have been like living during Old Testament times and having to follow through on these instructions to feel better.

Just like taking a shower after sweating from a hard day's work outside or other physical activity, you too can feel the cleansing of God's goodness on the inside. You too can feel as though God is showering His love over you and through you when you go to Him and confess your mistakes. Go, dear sister, and be cleansed and rejuvenated once more!

God, I'm so grateful I don't have to do anything
to earn Your forgiveness and love. Help me not
to look inward or downward on my own sins.
Instead, help me to look upward, toward the
freedom You provide through forgiveness.

Surety in Spring

"Oh, that we might know the LORD! Let us press on to know him. He will respond to us as surely as the arrival of dawn or the coming of rains in early spring."

HOSEA 6:3 NLT

Here the prophet clearly identifies seeking God—pressing on to know Him—with the coming of spring. His response is just as certain as the coming of spring. The Old Testament book of Hosea focuses on the themes of God's judgment but ultimate plans for restoration. The people of God during Hosea's time allowed themselves to be influenced by the pagan practices around them, engaging in pleasure-seeking activities and forgetting the goodness of God's provision for them up to the present time. God's love for them is revealed in His constant petitions for them to turn away from the things causing them pain. Whenever God allowed the winter of slavery on His people, He always brought spring. He tore but brought healing; broke the rebellious and then bound up the brokenhearted. The prophet laments the people's indifference and pleads with them to know their God again—to love Him as they did at first. God's response to those who press to know Him is as sure and as beautiful as the coming of early spring. His daughters have but to know Him and they will experience this surety.

My surety, let me press on in knowing You.
Hear the questions of my heart and respond in
the beauty and hope of renewal. Amen.

Wilderness Bloom

The wilderness and the wasteland shall be glad for them,
and the desert shall rejoice and blossom as the rose; it shall
blossom abundantly and rejoice, even with joy and singing.

ISAIAH 35:1–2 NKJV

After the bleakness of winter, a small crocus blooms and gives hope. We revel in its color and fragrance. We itch to wear sundresses, shorts, and sandals. There are times when our spiritual walk feels like a desert. There are few signs of life or progress, things are dry and brown, and it's hard to stay hopeful. But as Isaiah points out, God is our restorer and rainfall in a dry land. His glory makes our desert souls rejoice and blossom like the crocus.

The excitement you feel for the coming spring—have you ever felt that excited about your time with the Lord? Have you ever anticipated your daily devotion? Many times we treat scripture as a bandage or medicine; we only read and pray when we feel the need to. The Word of the Lord is vastly more powerful and abundant than a quick fix. You will never know the extent of scripture if you only read the red letters or Psalms. Scripture can make a desert heart blossom. Take time to analyze how and when you call upon the Lord. The majesty of our God is all around this spring. Are you worshipping the creature or the Creator?

Father, thank You for the blessing of spring!
I pray these coming days reveal the areas of my
heart that need Your tender care and tilling.

A Glimpse of Heaven

" 'He will wipe every tear from their eyes. There will be no more death' or mourning or crying or pain."

REVELATION 21:4 NIV

When the Israelites were preparing to cross into the Promised Land, they celebrated Passover. They had not been in the land long enough to cultivate it and create a rich harvest, but what they did eat they ate in anticipation of what God had promised them.

It is the same with heaven. Our time on earth is small and faded compared to the glory of heaven. While we are working through our difficulties here, we anticipate heaven, like the Israelites did the Promised Land.

Heaven will be a place of beauty. There will be no death, pain, fear, or impurity. God's creation will exist in the full glory He originally intended, not the wrecked-by-sin version we live in now. No sinfulness will mar it.

Relationships will deepen and expand and be deeply fulfilling without our sinfulness creating barriers between us and others. Rewards, restoration, and comfort are awaiting us. God will make it all up to us—all the loss, pain, and sorrow we experience in this world.

God gives us glimpses of heaven now to encourage us on our journey. He knows we can't see the whole picture, and He condescends to our frail humanity to give us what we need for the journey.

Heavenly Father, show us glimpses of heaven when the journey gets rough, and encourage us with what awaits us. Amen.

A Promised Healing

Behold, [in the future restored Jerusalem] I will lay
upon it health and healing, and I will cure them
and will reveal to them the abundance of peace
(prosperity, security, stability) and truth.

JEREMIAH 33:6 AMPC

Are you longing to be healed of an affliction? Mary Magdalene suffered with seven demons before Jesus touched her and restored her to life. Scripture doesn't tell us much about how, when, or where Jesus healed Mary. It does tell us that Mary, along with several other women, provided for and supported Jesus so that He could do what God had called Him to do. After Jesus healed her, she became one of his most ardent followers.

This woman, who had been tormented by Satan himself, became a walking testimony of the power of the light to dispel darkness: "The light shines in the darkness, and the darkness has not overcome it" (John 1:5 NIV).

Whether or not God chooses to cure you here on earth, one day He *will* restore you to total health. In heaven, our bodies will be perfect and no diseases will be allowed to touch us. We will live in peace and prosperity.

Such a promise should make us rejoice. Jesus will strengthen us for this life, whatever it may hold, and will one day turn on the light that will make the darkness scatter for all time. Hallelujah!

Heavenly Father, thank You for Your promise
of healing. Strengthen me as I walk this earth,
and give me hope as I look toward heaven.

The Want for Wonder

G. K. Chesterton said, "The world will never starve for want of wonders; but only for want of wonder." There are so many wonders in the world—places to see, goals to accomplish, exciting special effects—and yet many of us are still missing "awe."

The church is struggling too. Almost all of us—Christian and non-Christian alike—have grown up with a view of God as loving, accepting, and forgiving, and we have learned to take those attributes for granted. We've lost the wonder of His majesty.

In the early days of the apostles, many Jews repented and were baptized. They devoted themselves to teaching and fellowship, and "a deep sense of awe came over them all" (Acts 2:43 NLT). They were amazed by God!

We can regain our wonderment through reading God's Word. The more we learn about Him and our own condition, the more we can appreciate His love. Proverbs 25:2 (KJV) says, "It is the glory of God to conceal a thing: but the honour of kings is to search out a matter."

Is it time for you to examine the character of God in a fresh way? Pray today that He would open your eyes to His wonderful mysteries.

Father, restore in me the wonder of who You
are. It has been too long since I have found
myself amazed by Your love. Amen.

In His Presence

*In Your presence is fullness of joy; at Your
right hand are pleasures forevermore.*

PSALM 16:11 NKJV

Joseph Fort Newton said, "In the secret place of my heart there is a little door which, if I open and enter, I am in the presence of God."

What a striking depiction of the simplicity of meeting with God! Christians struggle to know the will of God, understand His Word, and control sin. But we only need to stop and enter in.

Newton's quote is reminiscent of *The Secret Garden* where Mary and Colin enter their world of beauty and friendship away from the oppressive world. They can play together and enjoy the work of the forgotten garden that they nourished back to life.

Similarly, we should long to enter through the secret door of our souls and spend time with the ultimate restorer. No wonder so many Christians have shallow roots and withering leaves—they spend no time with God!

Bible study and congregational worship may sustain you temporarily, but without the nutrients and connectedness to the vine, death is the ultimate destination—like cut flowers in a shop.

God is personal. He doesn't just want your work. He wants *you*, and that requires meeting with Him, talking with Him, gleaning from Him. In His presence, we are refreshed.

Lord, I say that I love You, but it has
been so long since I have spent time in
Your presence. Forgive me, and let us
come together right now. Amen.

I Will Praise Him Again

Why am I discouraged? Why is my heart so sad? I will put my hope in God! I will praise him again—my Savior and my God!

PSALM 42:5–6 NLT

When we allow the worries of this world to consume us, it's easy to fall into sadness and depression. Psalm 13:3 (NLT) is a very honest prayer: "Turn and answer me, O LORD my God! Restore the sparkle to my eyes, or I will die." Do you feel like the sparkle has left your eyes? Can others see the light of Christ in you, or are you known for being weighed down with sadness?

A life of faith isn't one where you walk around with a smile pasted on your face telling everyone that Jesus loves them even if you're not sure that's really true. A life of faith is marked by an authentic, loving relationship with God. You tell Him your burdens and He carries them for you. You're weighed down by sadness and stress, and God gives you rest. You take your suffering and depression to God, and He gives you a new heart!

What God wants from you is this: instead of telling every person but God your troubles, go to Him first. He will lovingly restore you and meet your every need. He will bring resources to you and show you the way! If you let go of trying to manipulate your circumstances and allow God to come to your rescue, He will!

God, forgive me for going to everyone but
You for help. I give You my needs and desires.
Please fill my heart with hope. Amen.

Cleaning the Pantry of Your Soul

Brethren, I count not myself to have apprehended: but this one thing I do, forgetting those things which are behind, and reaching forth unto those things which are before, I press toward the mark for the prize of the high calling of God in Christ Jesus. Let us therefore, as many as be perfect, be thus minded: and if in any thing ye be otherwise minded, God shall reveal even this unto you.

PHILIPPIANS 3:13–15 KJV

Businessman and minister John G. Lake once said, "Beloved, if any unholiness exists in the nature, it is not there by the consent of the Spirit of God. If unholiness is in your life, it is because your soul is giving consent to it, and you are retaining it. Let it go. Cast it out and let God have His way in your life."

As you grow in Christ, you will find that old thinking has to go to make room for the new understanding of God's desires and plans for your life. It's cleaning the pantry of your soul. Old mindsets and habits are like junk food or packages with expired dates. As you throw out the old, you find that the new thoughts and habits bring renewed life and strength in Christ.

Heavenly Father, I want to think Your thoughts and know Your ways. Help me to let go of the old ways and live in the new today. Amen.

The Gift of Sleep

In peace I will lie down and sleep.
PSALM 4:8 NLT

God infuses variety into our body clocks just like He does with other aspects of our personhood. So for every night owl, there is somewhere a morning lark or a hummingbird (those in the middle). And that way, all the jobs on earth get done and there is always someone awake with the needed energy and creativity. It would really be sad if no one could take the midnight shift at the hospital or if no one could get up at four in the morning to milk the cows!

Still, no matter the rhythm of one's internal clock, all of us need sleep. Our bodies require sleep to renew themselves and recharge for the next day. According to the National Sleep Foundation, while we are sleeping, tissue growth and repair occurs, energy is restored, hormones are released, appetite is balanced, and the immune system gets a charge. It is normal to spend about one-third of our lives sleeping.

And when you think about it, God did plan the nighttime for our benefit, right? In the beginning, He separated the darkness and light and gave each a place in the cycle of a twenty-four-hour day. And though He never needs to rest, we do. We cannot do the 24-7 thing; we weren't meant to. And as long as God sustains the earth, there will always be tomorrow in which to work.

Lord, let me praise You by getting the proper rest
for my body so that I may be at my optimum level
of energy and creativity for Your glory. Amen.

Fixed

All the broken and dislocated pieces of the universe—
people and things, animals and atoms—get properly fixed
and fit together in vibrant harmonies, all because of his
death, his blood that poured down from the cross.
COLOSSIANS 1:20 MSG

People often say we live in a broken world. And it's true. Our world is not the way God created it to be. When the first man and woman disobeyed, they broke that perfect relationship with God—they broke God's trust in them, and they broke the command He gave them. We could say they also broke His heart. And ever since, the perfection God meant for us to live in has been out of reach—shattered by sin.

Any parent who has had a child disobey and try to hide his disobedience will have had a taste of that kind of brokenness. If the betrayal is severe, it's hard to imagine a time when the relationship could be repaired. Every interaction is colored by the sorrow of the actions that tore away trust.

However, though God, in His perfect justice, had to punish humans for their disobedience, His perfect love for us sought to mend what was broken. He found that way of healing by sending His Son to die for us. Through Jesus Christ, every torn heart can be sewn back together, every broken promise redeemed, every destroyed relationship reborn. The world can be fixed.

Thank You, God! You gave us a way
to come back to You! Amen.

A Touch of Faith

*"Courage, daughter. You took a risk of
faith, and now you're well."*
MATTHEW 9:22 MSG

There once was a woman who'd been hemorrhaging for twelve years. She sought help from a myriad of physicians and spent all that she had, but her issue of blood was worse than ever before. Then one day she heard a healer named Jesus was coming to town. Although she was considered the lowest of the low, someone who shouldn't even be out in public, she decided to make her way through the crowd and reach out to this man. Risking all she had left, she came up behind Him and touched His garment, for she kept saying to herself, "If I can just touch his robe, I will be healed" (Mark 5:28 NLT). Instantly her bleeding stopped. But the story doesn't end there. Jesus immediately felt power flowing out of Him and demanded, "Who touched me?" (Mark 5:31 NLT). Shaking with fear, the woman confessed it had been her. Jesus responded with tenderness and encouragement, "Daughter, your faith has made you well. Go in peace. Your suffering is over" (Mark 5:34 NLT).

What issue have you needed Jesus' help with? What desperately bold exchange between your soul and Jesus have you kept secret? What story can you share with others to remind them of His power and tenderness, to give them a touch of faith?

Give me the courage, Jesus, to not just come
to You with all my issues but to share my story
with others, to touch them with my faith in
You and Your faithfulness to me. Amen.

Discover Your Dream Once Again

Restore unto me the joy of thy salvation;
and uphold me with thy free spirit.
PSALM 51:12 KJV

Have you ever looked at a small child and caught a glimpse of the possibilities of success that lay dormant within them? Perhaps you even picture just a little of who they might later become. Did you have a dream as a young person that has not yet been realized?

Life happens, and often those big dreams seem impossible. Maybe you went to school and started your career, maybe got married and started a family. Today that dream may be packed away in the garage, sitting on a shelf in the attic, or buried deep in a quiet, seldom touched part of your soul.

God has a plan. Even though you may have changed and gone in a different direction—that desire that He put within you can still be realized. The dream is still in there, and the ability to do what you once were passionate about can grow in your heart again. Dreams that God put in your heart are what make you who you were created to be. When you trust God to take your life and do with it what He purposed, He'll make your dreams a reality in His time. Just trust Him!

Heavenly Father, remind me of the dreams that
I have set aside. Those are not destroyed—
just forgotten. They are still within me, and I
am trusting You to restore them. Amen.

To Your Health!

Dear friend, I hope all is well with you and that you are as healthy in body as you are strong in spirit.

3 JOHN 2 NLT

God cares about your health. He took the time to mention it in His Word on multiple occasions. If you have any lingering doubts, just look at the many, many times Jesus healed the sick. His heart always went out to those who were struggling. With one touch, years of pain and agony disappeared. Maybe you're like many women and struggle with your health. Perhaps you're in chronic pain or live with an illness—diagnosed or undiagnosed. Today, be reminded that God cares! He longs to see you living life to your fullest potential. That same "touch" that healed the leper in Bible times is still available today, and God is no respecter of persons. What He's done for others He will do for you. Instead of giving in to fear (or thoughts that you're alone), reach out to Him. He loves you and longs to heal both your heart and body.

Thank You, God, for caring about my health. It's such a relief to know that You want me to be healthy, not just my heart and soul but my body as well. I'm so grateful for Your healing, Father. Amen.

Because

"Because you believed, it has happened."
MATTHEW 8:13 NLT

Quick: If you could have anything you wanted to happen right now, what would you ask for?

What came to your mind? Maybe you'd want healing for a loved one, or for yourself. Maybe you'd want one more day with someone who is gone. Maybe you'd ask for freedom from debt. Maybe you'd want a new job. Maybe you'd like a trip to an amusement park.

The centurion was a man with great responsibility and great courage. These officers in the Roman army would lead their men into battle—not hanging back and barking orders, but going first into the fighting, risking their lives to motivate their men to risk theirs.

The centurion risked his reputation to seek out Jesus and ask the Rabbi for help. It's not that he thought he was too good to be seen with Jesus. On the contrary, he didn't think himself worthy for Jesus even to come to his house.

But the man was confident about two things—Jesus' ability to heal and his own authority to give orders. And because he showed this faith to Jesus, the man's servant was healed.

What kind of faith do you have? What are you confident about? Have you shown this to Jesus? Seek Him out. Talk to Him. You never know what might happen just because you believe.

Lord Jesus, I come to You today to ask for
_____. I believe in You. Amen.

Do You Want to Be Healed?

When Jesus saw him lying there and learned
that he had been in this condition for a long time,
he asked him, "Do you want to get well?"

JOHN 5:6 NIV

The pool of Bethesda was where unwell people would go, waiting for an angel to stir the waters. The legend went that if someone made it into the water when the angel troubled the waters, that person would be healed. So Jesus' question doesn't seem to make sense. *Of course* the man wants to be healed. He's at a place where people go when they want to be healed.

When Jesus asks a question, it's not because He doesn't know the answer—He's all-knowing. He's asking it for our benefit.

The man's response to Jesus' question is also interesting. Instead of saying, "Yes, of course! Heal me!" he makes excuses as to why he hasn't been healed.

Isn't that like us? We want to be healed, but we make excuses why we aren't. Jesus is right there waiting to heal us of our wounds, our addictions, our bitterness—anything that keeps us from the best life He has for us. But He doesn't force Himself on us. He asks us, "Do you want to be healed?" We must reach out to Him. We must exercise our faith in Him.

Lord Jesus, thank You for Your great love for us.
Give us the courage to reach out to You for our
healing. Help us move past our excuses and
reach for that best life You have for us. Amen.

A Love Song

I will sing of the LORD's unfailing love forever!
Young and old will hear of your faithfulness.
PSALM 89:1 NLT

A changed heart is a happy heart, one filled with a new song, ready to be sung. Maybe you can relate. You've been through changes. Major transformations have taken place, not just in your heart, but in your thinking as well. God has lifted your feet from the miry clay and placed them on a rock. He's brought you through the valley to a season of great joy.

Now you want to share the news with everyone you meet. Your testimony leads the way as you have conversation after conversation with friends, family, coworkers, and neighbors. You can't help it. You're so grateful at all God has done that you want others to see His goodness too.

Today why not go even further? Don't just spread your joy in conversation. Sing praises to the Lord! Let your mouth sing—and others hear—what your heart is already celebrating!

Lord, I choose to praise You today! You're so worthy, Father! I will not just share the stories of what You've done in my life—how You've changed and transformed me, re-created me, given me a new sense of purpose and wonder. But with my whole heart I will praise You in song, telling all of Your unfailing and forever love. Amen.

Dreamer

"In the last days, God says, I will pour out my Spirit on all people. Your sons and daughters will prophesy, your young men will see visions, your old men will dream dreams."

ACTS 2:17 NIV

Ah, the dreamer! She sees all of life's possibilities and believes every dream can come true. And she has no shortage of dreams either. Her creativity knows no bounds. She's got an idea a minute. Don't believe it? Just ask her! Perhaps you can relate to this fun woman of God. Maybe you're a dreamer too. If so, you must surely enjoy seeing those once-upon-a-time ideas come to fruition. How excited the Lord must be when He peers inside the hearts of his dreamer daughters. He placed that creative bent inside of them, after all. Today, spend some time glancing back at some of the dreams God placed in your heart. Have all of them come true? If not, maybe it's time to reawaken a few!

I don't mind admitting I've always been a dreamer,
Lord. I have plans. Ideas. Creative streaks. I know
You placed these dreams inside of me, and I
can't wait to see which ones will come to fruition.
Thanks for entrusting them to me! Amen.

A Woman's Faith

*Then Jesus said to her, "Woman, you have
great faith! Your request is granted." And her
daughter was healed at that moment.*

MATTHEW 15:28 NIV

This Canaanite woman has a demon-possessed daughter. She and her daughter are descendants of the people Joshua and Israel drove out of the Promised Land due to their sin.

Jesus' treatment of this woman is puzzling at first. He begins by ignoring her pleas. But she keeps following Him and His disciples. Then when He does talk to her, He seems to imply that she is a dog and doesn't deserve His attention.

But Jesus is doing something much bigger here. In treating her the way that any Jewish man would, He is giving her an opportunity to express her faith in Him, something her heritage has denied her. Her determination proves the strength of her faith.

He is delighted to grant her request. He commends her faith, and He uses the same term of endearment, *woman*, that He used with His mother at the wedding where He turned water into wine. Jesus is proving to her that heritage doesn't determine her relationship with God; her faith does.

He invites you as His daughter to come to Him and relate to Him in a personal and loving way. Let Him show you how much He loves and values you.

Lord Jesus, thank You for loving us, for lifting us
up beyond our earthly heritage and giving us
immeasurable value in Your eyes. Amen.

Heavenly Vision

*" 'He will wipe every tear from their eyes. There will be
no more death' or mourning or crying or pain, for the
old order of things has passed away." He who was seated
on the throne said, "I am making everything new!"*

REVELATION 21:4–5 NIV

Longing for heaven is a learned longing. How could it be natural
when so much beauty exists on this earth for us to see, taste, and
touch? As wonderful as this short life can be, it will not compare
to what awaits us—seeing the loveliness of the Savior with our
own eyes and hearing His voice with our ears, knowing that we
will never part from Him.

In His presence, all imperfection, pain, and sadness will
vanish, and the earth will be remade. We will be reunited with
our loved ones in Christ who were separated from us on earth by
death or distance. The expectation of that day helps us persevere
through the hurt and brokenness of the present. Knowing that
complete peace and joy lie ahead gives us courage.

Even now, Christ's work isn't on hold—He is making us new
by renewing our hearts and strength; He is teaching us how to
love as He loves in order to draw more people to Himself. Hold
this world loosely, for it will fade in the light of the Savior's face.
He who calls us beloved is coming again soon!

Dear heavenly Father, thank You that You gave
us the hope of heaven when You sent Jesus.
Give me a heart that longs for heaven and
longs for Your presence even more. Amen.

A Dash of Faith

*But Jesus overheard them and said to Jairus,
"Don't be afraid. Just have faith."*
MARK 5:36 NLT

"Don't be afraid and just have faith"—wouldn't it be nice if your faith walk seemed that easy?

At times, it's easier said than done, right? Yet as Jesus was healing people, it appeared that the primary ingredient, perhaps the *only* ingredient, those individuals needed was a dash of faith. That dash was enough to heal, redeem, and restore the lives of individuals who had been suffering for *years*.

Perhaps all you need today is fearless faith. Not fix it yourself, find the strength and faith from within. Just fearless faith in who God is, and says He is, in your life. A fearless, expectant faith that He will heal, redeem, and restore you. Perhaps adopt the psalmist's attitude: "Hope in God and wait expectantly for Him, for I shall yet praise Him, Who is the help of my countenance, and my God" (Psalm 42:11 AMPC).

Today as you reflect on these passages, ask God to give you a dash of faith where you need it the most and expect Him to work wonders in your life.

Lord, I want faith that is childlike but can also move mountains! Help me not to muster up enough willpower or gumption within myself, but to have faith that is filled with Your divine strength and courage.

In the Storm

*When they climbed back into the boat, the wind
stopped. Then the disciples worshiped him.
"You really are the Son of God!" they exclaimed.*

MATTHEW 14:32–33 NLT

This was not the first supernatural show the disciples had attended. They had seen Jesus heal many. They had just handed out dinners—which Jesus had created from some bread and fish—to more than five thousand people. They had even watched Jesus calm a storm on a lake before. They were intimately acquainted with the power of this man. They felt the press of the crowds of people seeking His healing touch. They picked up the leftovers from His miracle meals. Their faces were splashed with the waves that He then silenced. Yet here they are again—scared by a storm.

At least Peter knew Jesus' voice.

At least Peter trusted Jesus enough to step onto the waves.

And Jesus met him on the way.

We are so very much like those quaking disciples—knowing full well what our God is capable of, and yet still needing to see the wind stopped before we can trust Him. But if we just have at least enough courage to stick our toes into the stormy waters, we might feel the blessing of Jesus reaching down and rescuing us. . .again.

Jesus, my Lord, help me trust You enough
to get out of the boat! Amen.

Plan to Trust

The LORD knows all human plans; he knows that they are futile.
PSALM 94:11 NIV

Ever have your plans blow up in your face? In 1 Kings 12, King Jeroboam of Israel had a pretty good plan to keep his kingship out of trouble, but it backfired in a big way. God had promised a throne for Jeroboam and his descendants if he was obedient to His commands, but Jeroboam was worried about one little detail—the temple in Jerusalem. He feared that if his people traveled to Judah to worship, they would defect to King Rehoboam, his rival. So Jeroboam made golden calves in Israel as a stand-in for the temple. As did Aaron, Jeroboam severely disobeyed God's commands by doing this, and while it didn't happen immediately, his kingly line disintegrated.

Certainly you have made plans for a secure life: working toward a full savings account or keeping your family healthy or other good goals. But what's driving your plans—fear of the future or faith that God's grace will be there for you in the future? Every Christian struggles with this. But relying on anything for security apart from God never ends well. . .and it puts distance between you and Him. Where is fear steering your way? Pour out your worries to Him, and He will restore your heart with His abiding peace (see John 16:33).

Jesus, help me plan to trust You; teach my heart
to expect Your grace in what's ahead.

Help in Doubt

For the Lord is great and greatly to be praised;
He is to be feared above all gods.
PSALM 96:4 NKJV

When the widow's son was brought back to life, she declared to Elijah, "Now by this I know that you are a man of God, and that the word of the Lord in your mouth is the truth" (1 Kings 17:24 NKJV).

It's interesting that she didn't say this after Elijah showed her the miracle of the flour and oil. Perhaps she'd wondered, *Was that really the God of Israel who rescued us from starving? Maybe it was one of the local gods.* But she put her full trust in Jehovah when her son was restored to her; no other god could reverse death's curse.

Maybe pain is running rampant in your life or you are looking at what's happening in the world and wondering where God even is. But He's here, and He's powerful—the God who brought the widow's boy back from the dead also raised your Savior. . .and resurrected your heart to new life.

When doubt strikes and death seems triumphant, immerse yourself in His truth. Don't fear your doubt, for God doesn't; abiding in Christ sometimes looks more like clawing to catch hold of Him. Seek Him; He will show you the truth the widow knew—that He is present and mighty—and fill your heart with what it needs.

Father, thank You for helping me when doubt strikes.

Celebrate Justice. . .and Grace

So the king died and was brought to Samaria, and
they buried him there. They washed the chariot
at a pool in Samaria. . .and the dogs licked up his
blood, as the word of the LORD had declared.

1 KINGS 22:37–38 NIV

The prophecy made Ahab quake in his sandals—his kingly line would fall, and the dogs would lap up his blood (see 1 Kings 21:19–22). Well aware of the trouble he was in, Ahab tried to escape his fate by dressing up like a common soldier when he went to battle, but an arrow drawn "at random" caught him "between the sections of his armor" (1 Kings 22:34 NIV), showing that God's justice cannot be fooled.

Maybe you did a little victory dance when you read that Ahab got what he deserved. But. . .have you considered your sins' consequences recently? Surely you haven't stolen and committed murder as Ahab did, but sin in any form creates distance between you and God and hurts your fellow man. And its consequences reverberate. So celebrate His justice, but be sure to fall on His grace.

As you come into God's presence through Jesus, confess your sins with reverence and awe for His unfathomable holiness and grace, and be restored. Humbly thank Him for the forgiveness He gave in Christ—because you have only escaped the true weight of justice through grace.

Father, let me never forget that my relationship
with You was bought by Jesus' sacrifice.

The Shield of Faith

*Above all, taking the shield of faith, wherewith ye shall
be able to quench all the fiery darts of the wicked.*

EPHESIANS 6:16 KJV

When Paul wrote to the church at Ephesus about the shield of
faith, he used the word *thureos*, which means "door." Roman
soldiers' shields were large, rectangular, and door sized. In other
words, they covered every single part of the soldier's body. It's
the same with our faith. The salvation we've been given in Christ
covers us from head to toe. And because He is lavish in love and
steadfast in keeping His promises, we'll always have enough for
every situation we encounter.

The Roman soldiers' shields had one other distinctive quality:
they were made of several hides of leather sewn together. This
meant that every morning, a soldier would have to rub oil into
the shield to keep it pliable and to prevent it from drying out and
cracking. This daily renewal was the difference between life and
death. . .literally!

In our own faith walk, we must daily allow God's Holy Spirit
to refill and reenergize us. The Spirit replenishes our joy, rebuilds
our faith, and redirects our thoughts so that we can live boldly
and courageously for Jesus. This raises the question: What have
we done today to oil our shields? Let's not get complacent and
allow distractions to deter us from our duty! In Christ, we have
a true shield that won't ever let us down. Praise the Lord!

Lord, thank You for Your Word and all the
riches I find there. Give me the discipline
to come to You regularly for refilling.

Drawing Near

For who in the skies above can compare with the LORD?
Who is like the LORD among the heavenly beings?
PSALM 89:6 NIV

In John 13 Jesus caused no small amount of consternation as He, the esteemed teacher, took on a Jewish household's lowliest job to wash His disciples' feet. Though a shock (to Peter especially), this was just one of many humbling acts that Jesus did in His earthly life. There is no one like Him—"he is more awesome than all who surround him" (Psalm 89:7 NIV)—yet Jesus came to dwell with His creation, to display His perfect love by walking with humanity side by side. The complete picture of His humility is that Jesus "loved [His followers] to the end" (John 13:1 NIV) by laying down His perfect life to redeem all humankind's imperfections.

Have you pondered how Jesus "washes" your feet? He cleansed you by His saving work, yet does confessing your sin make you shrink back from prayer?

Do not hang back as Peter did at first. Your big brother Jesus invites you to prop up your feet and let Him see your dirty, well-worn soles—no sin of yours is too dark, no hurt too scarred, for Him to heal. Confess and repent before your Savior, and feel His gentle, loving, and protective hands washing you clean.

Jesus, thank You for humbling Yourself so I
can draw near and be renewed by You.

Stubborn

But when Pharaoh saw that relief had come,
he became stubborn. He refused to listen to Moses
and Aaron, just as the LORD had predicted.

EXODUS 8:15 NLT

By this time in Pharaoh's story, he must have known something was rotten in Egypt. Aaron's staff had become a serpent, right before his eyes. And the Egyptians had been digging for water, since their rivers turned to blood. Now he pulled back his sheets and found frogs in his bed!

But even as the plagues on his land became worse and worse, even when his own magicians claimed, "This is the finger of God!" (Exodus 8:19 NLT), even after destruction rained down on his land, Pharaoh was resolute. He refused to let the people of Israel leave.

Why? Because they were his.

So often we hold on tightly to the things in our possession, the relationships we are tied up in, the emotional rides we have ridden for years—we hold on so tightly, even if it hurts our own hands, or our hearts. We just don't want to admit defeat. Or we want to believe that we can somehow perform a miracle ourselves and change what's hurting us into something that heals. But only God can heal. And only God can work these kinds of miracles. And if God is telling you to let go, then it's time to let go.

**Lord, help me to release anything that
is keeping me from You. Amen.**

Perfect Rest

Come to Me, all you who labor and are heavy-laden
and overburdened, and I will cause you to rest.
[I will ease and relieve and refresh your souls.]
MATTHEW 11:28 AMPC

One day the crowds pushed against Jesus as He taught. So, instead of allowing them to push Him into the deeper waters of the Sea of Galilee lapping at His feet, He got into one of the fishing vessels His disciples owned. When the evening came, He asked His disciples to take Him to the other side of the lake. So they did. While the majority of the crowd couldn't follow Him, a few did who had boats.

Jesus, tired from the day's teaching, healing, and casting out demons, went to the back of the boat and fell asleep. Even when a severe storm blew up, He slept on. Finally, afraid the huge waves would swamp the ship, the disciples woke Jesus with their shouting: "Teacher, don't you care that we're going to drown?" (Mark 4:38 NLT).

Jesus woke, heard the disciples' fear, and rebuked the wind and waves, and they instantly calmed. This is the kind of rest the Lord desires to give to His children when He said, "Come to Me, all you who labor and are heavy-laden and overburdened."

When we go to Him for rest, He eases, relieves, and refreshes our souls. He gives the best kind of refreshment we could ever wish for.

Father, please remove the burden that
weighs me down and give the rest that
eases, relieves, and refreshes my soul.

Springs of Water

"The LORD will guide you always; he will satisfy your needs in a sun-scorched land and will strengthen your frame. You will be like a well-watered garden, like a spring whose waters never fail."

ISAIAH 58:11 NIV

Without life-giving water, a garden will dry up, eventually turn to dust, and blow away. In areas where springs stop bubbling, life stagnates. You want your life to be like a well-watered garden, bearing fruit day after day. You want to be like a cool, bubbling spring, flowing and nurturing everything around you.

Abiding close to the heart of God is the secret to being replenished by the master gardener. God knows that living apart from Him leaves you with scorched places within. Time with Him renews you with waters that never fail. No matter your circumstances, step into the lush oasis created by God for those who seek Him. Linger there, gaining refreshment of soul and clarity of mind.

God desires His children to love each other well. When you treat others by God's standards of justice, He promotes healing and strength in your life as described in this chapter of Isaiah.

Physical strength provides stamina and health to dry bones. Strength of spirit allows you to be brave in uncertainty. The strength God provides is a sure and solid power. It will not leave you faltering or failing—but ever fruitful and flowing.

God, thank You, my master gardener,
for tending me with Your loving hand.

Jesus, the Healer

"Since the world began it has been unheard of that anyone opened the eyes of one who was born blind. If this Man were not from God, He could do nothing."

JOHN 9:32–33 NKJV

The man was blind, and then he could see. The Pharisees questioned him thoroughly regarding this miracle Jesus had performed. The man did not understand fully who Jesus was. But he understood this: *he was blind, and then he could see!*

He said to the Pharisees that no one in the history of the world had done such a thing—opened the eyes of one born blind. He then pointed out that if this man Jesus were not from God, He would not have been able to do this.

It didn't take an Ivy League education to figure that out. But the religious leaders of the day were, in fact, the blind ones in the story. They didn't want to believe Jesus was the long-awaited Messiah. They were looking for pageantry and grandeur, not a carpenter's son from Nazareth who didn't even own His own home.

Think about your own life. What blessing has come to you that clearly could have come only from the hand of God? Ask Him to heal your life. After all, He's the Son of God. All things are possible through Christ.

Jesus, You gave the blind sight and caused the lame to walk. Heal that which is broken in me as well. Amen.

Remarkable Growth

Then He said, "What is the kingdom of God like? And to what shall I compare it? It is like a mustard seed, which a man took and put in his garden; and it grew and became a large tree, and the birds of the air nested in its branches."
LUKE 13:18–19 NKJV

A mustard seed is a tiny thing—so small that you might look right past it and not see it at all. And yet, from that tiny seed grows a magnificent tree. The same is true with our faith. God can take even the smallest grain of faith and use it to bring about the greatest miracles. Mountains can be moved. Rivers crossed. Addictions broken. Brokenness healed. Mourning lifted.

What are you believing God for today? Does your faith feel small? Trust Him, even in your weakest moments, to accomplish great things. He has the ability to take the smallest thing and grow it beyond your wildest imagination. Best of all, He always carries through on His promises. If He said it, He will most certainly do it.

I have to admit it, Lord, I sometimes doubt the process. I see a tiny mustard seed and have a hard time imagining it blossoming into a magnificent tree. Today, Father, I place every "small" thing into Your hands and trust that You will bring all things to fruition in my life. You're growing me into a mighty woman, and I choose to trust You during the process. Amen.

Renew Your Strength

But those who wait for the Lord [who expect, look for,
and hope in Him] shall change and renew their strength
and power; they shall lift their wings and mount up [close to
God] as eagles [mount up to the sun]; they shall run and not
be weary, they shall walk and not faint or become tired.

ISAIAH 40:31 AMPC

Andrew Murray was a South African writer, teacher, and Christian pastor in the late 1900s who captured the heart of prayer with these words about Jesus: "While others still slept, He went away to pray and to renew His strength in communion with His Father. He had need of this, otherwise He would not have been ready for the new day. The holy work of delivering souls demands constant renewal through fellowship with God."

Each day you give a part of yourself to that day—spiritually, emotionally, physically, financially, and socially. Within each of those areas of life, you need to refuel. Spiritually, the only way to recharge is a renewal that comes from God. Waiting for a fresh outpouring of His life-giving Spirit brings a newness and a fresh perspective on all the other areas of your life. Give your best each day by drawing on the strength of your heavenly Father and spending time with Him.

Heavenly Father, Your Word and prayer are
strength to my soul. Renew me and pour
Your life into me. Fill me with Your power and
give me courage for a new day. Amen.

Even When You Don't See, Believe

Yet God has made everything beautiful for its own time. He has planted eternity in the human heart, but even so, people cannot see the whole scope of God's work from beginning to end.
ECCLESIASTES 3:11 NLT

Seeing your loved ones suffer is difficult. Mothers especially know this, for good mothers tend to feel their own child's pain, whether it's caused by physical addiction, illness or injury, divorce or other loss, spiritual doubt or confusion, financial bankruptcy or debt, or mental issues—the list can go on and on.

The concern you, as a woman, have for others can almost consume you. You imagine a thousand things that could come from the current situation and another thousand ways you could possibly fix things. You find yourself wanting to wrap your arms around your loved one and tell that person it's going to be okay. But deep down you know it's going to hurt for a while.

Chin up, woman. You know God is at work behind the scenes. He makes all things beautiful in His time. He is there to heal your loved one—and you. Yes, God will make it beautiful again. You just have to believe it till you see it.

God, You are making all things beautiful in Your time. Amid the turmoil in my life and the lives of those I love, I will trust You.

Heart of Gold

Create in me a pure heart, O God,
and renew a steadfast spirit within me.
PSALM 51:10 NIV

Do you remember playing with modeling clay when you were a child? You could mold a blob into whatever you wanted—an animal, a flower, a person, wherever your mood took you. Or maybe you remember building things with blocks. Again, you had the ability and freedom to create something amazing from individual interlocking blocks. But God, the master craftsman, has the ability to create something much more magnificent—a pure heart within you!

Yet that's not all! David tells us that the almighty God has the ability to "renew a right, persevering, and steadfast *spirit* within" (Psalm 51:10 AMPC, emphasis added) you.

No matter what you've done or where you've been, God renews you just as He has renewed "the ruined cities that have been devastated for generations" (Isaiah 61:4 NIV). He can restore to you "the joy of your salvation and grant [you] a willing spirit" (Psalm 51:12 NIV), one that will sustain you!

What a blessing! A pure heart and steadfast spirit and joy—all you need for a life of grace and happiness. It is yours for the asking. So why not ask today?

Dear God, I ask that You create a pure heart within me, renew and fortify my spirit, forgiving me my failures and sins. And, Lord, I pray You would also restore the joy of my salvation and bless me with a willing spirit. Amen.

Tried and True

When Peter preached a sermon at Pentecost, he drew from the
scriptures, which had stood the test of time. Peter quoted David's
inspired words: "I saw the Lord always before me. Because he is
at my right hand, I will not be shaken. Therefore my heart is glad
and my tongue rejoices; my body also will rest in hope, because
you will not abandon me to the realm of the dead.... You will fill
me with joy in your presence" (Acts 2:25–28 NIV). People were
yearning for stability, for peace, hope, and joy. David was a king
who had seen much trouble in his life, some self-inflicted, some
not. Yet he was a man who loved God despite the trouble. And he
was a child of God—God, who had held him through the trouble.
Because God was near, David would not be shaken.

God's promise of a restored relationship with Him was not
for David alone. It is to everyone He calls to Himself. He wants to
be ever before us, ever at our side, so that we will not be shaken.
That's a promise that stands the test of time.

God, sometimes I depend on temporary
things to provide stability. Open my eyes to
see You—my eternal rock—before me.

Emptiness

"You have made known to me the paths of life;
you will fill me with joy in your presence."
ACTS 2:28 NIV

Imagine you're looking at a full-to-the-brim rain barrel. You've been in a season of abundant rain. It never occurs to you that a dry season might be around the corner.

Now picture yourself, weeks later, staring down into the barrel, noticing that it's bone dry. Drought has taken its toll. Now you have a picture of what it's like when you go through a season of spiritual wholeness and spiritual drought. Your rain barrel—your heart—is only as full as what's poured into it.

Did you realize that God can refill your heart with just one word? When He sees that your well is running dry, it breaks His heart. The only solution is to run into His arms and ask for a fresh outpouring of His holy water, the kind that will replenish your soul and give you the nourishment you need to move forward in Him.

It's up to you. God is waiting to meet with you. His everlasting water is prepped and ready to be poured out on you. All you need to do. . .is run to Him.

Father, I've been blaming my dry spell on so many different things: Exhaustion. Frustration. You name it, I've pointed the finger at it. Lord, I need the kind of water that You provide—the kind that will never run dry. Today, Lord, I run into Your arms, ready to be refreshed!

Power Filled

How mighty is our God! How utterly powerful! At His command the universe was formed out of nothingness. In His presence the same creation shakes: "The earth sees and trembles. The mountains melt like wax before the LORD, before the Lord of all the earth" (Psalm 97:4–5 ESV).

That same powerful God chooses to funnel His power into us. Imagine! His power that makes the earth tremble and mountains melt is the power that makes us new. A beggar in Jerusalem experienced this firsthand. The man had been unable to walk since birth and was carried to the temple each day, where he would remain all day, asking for alms. But God performed a miracle through Peter and John—the man's legs were healed *instantly*.

Peter was just as quick to give credit where credit was due. He told the crowd it wasn't his healing power that did the miracle, rather it was God who made the lame beggar strong (Acts 3:12, 16). It is our God also who restores us, who strengthens us, who steadies us. It is our God who makes crippled souls whole to dance and praise Him. Imagine.

Lord, emotionally, I feel like a blob on the floor. I turn to You, the one whose power can make me stand again.

Receptive

And Jesus said, "All right, receive your sight! Your faith has healed you." Instantly the man could see, and he followed Jesus, praising God. And all who saw it praised God, too.

LUKE 18:42–43 NLT

Receive. What an interesting word. When we're handed a gift, we must take it into our hands to receive it. The same is true when it comes to the things of God. He stands ready to answer our prayers, but asks, "Are you ready?" When we answer with a triumphant, "Yes!" He responds with the words: "Then, receive!"

How do we get into "receptive" mode? What role do we play? We must empty our hands of anything we've been holding on to, then lift them, palms extended, to Him. We have to set our hearts and mind on Him, not on the gifts He's pouring out. Most of all, we have to praise Him—to have a heart of thanksgiving—even before the gifts arrive.

What are you waiting on today? Prepare your heart. Put a song of praise on your lips. Get ready to receive from on high.

A receptive heart is a trusting heart, Lord! That's the kind of heart I want to have. May I be so ready, so filled with anticipation of what You're about to do, that my heart is wide open to the miraculous. I can't wait to see what You have in store, Father! Amen.

A Ready Boat

Jesus went off with his disciples to the sea to get away. But a huge crowd from Galilee trailed after them. . . . He told his disciples to get a boat ready so he wouldn't be trampled by the crowd.

MARK 3:7–9 MSG

Jesus was having one of those days. A day when no matter where He went, He faced a myriad of people.

He tried to get away from the crowd. But the crowds continued to follow Him. They'd heard all about how He'd healed many—spiritually, emotionally, mentally, physically. Some wanted to witness His work. Others wanted to receive their own healing.

Thus, amid this swarm of people, Jesus asked His disciples to have a boat ready for Him, a safe haven where He could take refuge when the pressure was too great.

What safe haven do you have standing by? Where is your refuge, the place you can escape to when you need some space?

Jesus understands that you will, from time to time, need a retreat. So why not ask Him what the perfect place would be for you, a place that would always be standing by, at the ready?

Lord Jesus, help me find my own readied boat,
a place where I can run to when I need some
breathing room. Help me find a refuge where I
can recharge and be renewed by You. Amen.

Seriously?

I urge you to live a life worthy of the calling you have received. Be completely humble and gentle; be patient, bearing with one another in love. Make every effort to keep the unity of the Spirit through the bond of peace.

EPHESIANS 4:1–3 NIV

Do you have a friend, relative, or coworker who you feel is trying to drive you crazy? At times, do you think you need to throw your hands in the air and walk away. . .or maybe get in that person's face and tell it like it is? While there are times for confrontation and discussion of conflicts, often at the center of the problem is "me." I am my problem. Perhaps we need to look in the mirror and evaluate the situation to see where we can improve.

Scripture encourages us to be humble, gentle, and patient. Then to bear one another in love. Wow! Huge directions. Doesn't the Lord get it? Doesn't He see how. . . Wait. Yes, He does. He understands full well we cannot accomplish these tasks in our own strength. That's why He has given us the Holy Spirit. So we can lean on Him to guide us to peace.

As we walk through the days ahead, let us keep our eyes lifted, which removes the problems from our sight. Maybe not from our lives, but the focus isn't necessarily on the difficulty—be it human or otherwise. Our focus is on Jesus. And with His help, we can conquer all.

Father God, refresh the Holy Spirit within me. Let me feel His presence. Amen.

Don't Forget

Praise the LORD, my soul; all my inmost being, praise his holy name. Praise the LORD, my soul, and forget not all his benefits.
PSALM 103:1–2 NIV

The phrase *praise the Lord* is found scores of times in the Psalms, whether things were good—*or bad*. How is praise possible when our world is in turmoil? How is praise possible when all that meets our eyes is negative? We must choose to keep God's blessings in mind, to think on all God does. That's what David did. He told his soul to praise and to forget not. . . .

Forget not that God forgives every sin—even the ones we have a hard time letting go of ourselves. Forget not that God heals us, body and soul. Forget not that God redeems lives from the deep, dank, dark pit. Forget not that God then crowns us with love, with compassion that we don't deserve but that we need desperately. Forget not that God satisfies our desires with good things—yes, the *best* things—so that we are renewed like eagles soaring high above it all. (See Psalm 103:3–5.)

In light of God's benefits, nothing on earth can douse our praise if we don't allow it. And nothing on earth can take God's benefits away.

God, whatever happens around me or to me,
Your benefits are for sure. Praise the Lord,
my soul—and there is so much to praise You for!

Continually Satisfied

Jesus replied, "If you only knew the gift God has for you and who you are speaking to, you would ask me, and I would give you living water."

JOHN 4:10 NLT

In the Old Testament, the people of God are continually searching for a place to belong. They want to live in peace, raise their families, tend their land, and leave a legacy for the next generation. Over and over, all these things seem denied to them. In fact, in Psalm 78, the history of the Israelites is told—and it's a tale of wandering indeed. Both literally and spiritually.

In New Testament days, the Samaritans were living proof that often the quest for happiness did not turn out well. The result of intermarriage, the people of Samaria were considered "dogs" by full Jews. And the Samaritans returned the favor by hating the Hebrews as well.

When Jesus purposely stopped by Jacob's well to talk to a Samaritan woman, He acted completely out of character for a Jewish man. But He went a step further. He even offered her the same redemption He came to bring to His own people. He invited her to drink the living water of relationship with God. He welcomed her to enjoy fulfillment with everyone else who puts their trust in Him.

Father, often I forget how great a gift it is
that I have a relationship with You to satisfy
my deep longing! Thank You for this continual
drink of refreshing, living water. Amen.

All Things New

*In the beginning God created the heavens and the
earth. The earth was formless and empty, and
darkness covered the deep waters. And the Spirit of
God was hovering over the surface of the waters.*

GENESIS 1:1–2 NLT

Don't you wish you could have peeked over the veil during creation week? God took nothing. . .and created everything. Wow! The earth, in its initial stage, was formless and empty—totally dark. Deep waters covered it all. But here's the really cool part: the Spirit of God hovered over the surface of the waters.

Pause to think about that for a moment. When the Creator created, the Spirit hovered over what He was spinning into creation. The same thing is true today. When He re-created you (when you were born again), the Spirit of God played a key role. And when you create (whether a work of art, a plan, or a cake) the Spirit of God hovers over that too.

When you realize the Holy Spirit is ever present in your life, everything changes! There's no need to be shaken when God Himself shows up. And though you may feel formless and empty at times, just as the earth was in its initial stages, the incoming Spirit brings life where there was no life and hope where there was no hope.

What are you creating today? Expect the Holy Spirit to show up and show off.

Lord, I'm so grateful for Your Spirit.
Thank You for hovering over the things
You're creating through me. Amen.

Finding Calm

But I have calmed and quieted myself, I am like a weaned
child with its mother; like a weaned child I am content.

PSALM 131:2 NIV

There are a couple of apps you can purchase on a smartphone
that promise calm. They include soft music, white noise and rain
sounds, meditation and breathing exercises. The makers of these
apps know what a lot of the women in this world need—a chance
to escape, to relax and recharge, to find contentment. Although
you may not be able to control your circumstances, you can try
to get a rein on your emotions.

Like an anxious child who only wants her mother, your heart
longs for a place of comfort, peace, and contentment. Although
you know there are some things in this world that can give you
momentary peace and comfort, where can you go for something
long lasting?

Go to God. He yearns to be that source of long-lasting calm
you need. He wants you to come into His presence for comfort,
peace, and contentment. This type of calm is unshakable and
immoveable because it comes straight from God. It will never
fade away or falter.

To obtain that kind of calm, all you need to do is put your
faith and trust in the Lord. Because when you trust that God
is working in your life now, you aren't anxious for your future.

Lord, thank You for the everlasting calm
You provide when I'm anxious. Amen.

Go in Peace

The king's officer pleaded with Him, Sir, do come down
at once before my little child is dead! Jesus answered
him, Go in peace; your son will live! And the man put
his trust in what Jesus said and started home.

JOHN 4:49–50 AMPC

A Roman official's son was near death. So the officer approached Jesus and begged Him to come home with him so He could put His hands on the child and heal him. But Jesus told the king's man not to be anxious, to go home in peace, because his son would indeed live.

At that very moment, the officer took Jesus at His word. He believed what He said was reality. *He trusted Him.* And so the king's man started back home. On his way there, his servants came to tell him the boy had indeed recovered—at the same moment that Jesus had told the man, "Go in peace; your son will live!"

Put no limits on what Jesus and His words can do in your life. There's no amount of time or space He cannot reach across with His power. Believe in His words, that things are indeed just as He says they are. Trust what He tells you; then go in peace, knowing His truth is yours.

Lord, with You there are no limits. You can reach across time and space. I believe and trust in what You say.
I go in peace, knowing Your truths are my truths.

From Sickbed to Servant's Heart

And when Jesus entered Peter's house, he saw his mother-in-law lying sick with a fever. He touched her hand, and the fever left her, and she rose and began to serve him.

MATTHEW 8:14–15 ESV

Peter's mother-in-law was terribly ill on the day that Jesus came by for a visit. If you've ever been down for the count with the flu or other feverish bug, you can imagine how she was feeling— definitely not up to a houseguest.

Oh, but this guest was different from all the others. He walked in and reached to touch her hand, and the fever immediately left her. (Can you imagine?) She jumped up out of bed and did what any hostess would do—began to serve Him.

Maybe you've been through a season of illness or pain and have wished Jesus would sweep in and touch you like that. You've prayed for instantaneous healing, but it didn't come in such a sweeping, awe-inspiring way.

Don't give up. Don't let the wait shake your faith. Just remember that one gentle touch from the Savior was enough to change absolutely everything. Keep your focus on Him until that moment comes.

I won't give up, Lord. I'm ready to rise from this sickbed and do great things for You. Touch me, I pray. Amen.

Have You Thanked Someone Today?

They have been a wonderful encouragement
to me, as they have been to you.
1 CORINTHIANS 16:18 NLT

Paul wrote to the Corinthian church, explaining how Stephanas and his family were the first converts in Achaia and how they devoted themselves to serving others. He reminded them that when Stephanas, Fortunatus, and Achaicus arrived in Corinth, they supplied whatever needs the people had and they "refreshed my spirit and yours" (1 Corinthians 16:18 NIV).

When true believers serve, they serve from the heart, not an inward desire for outward praise. This is what Stephanas did, yet Paul still prompted the church to show appreciation for God's servant and what he did for them.

Do you ever feel taken advantage of? Do you labor and receive little to no recognition? As God's servants, we work because we love Christ; yet an occasional display of appreciation is always. . .well, appreciated. That's what Paul communicated. "Hey guys, let's encourage our brothers through showing our appreciation to them for all they did for us!"

Paul's suggestion holds true today. Thank someone who has refreshed your spirit. It will encourage them and you to keep persevering on life's pathway.

Lord, encourage me to show my appreciation
to those who have touched my life with
Your love and grace. Amen.

Be on Your Way

*"When you knock on a door, be courteous in your greeting.
If they welcome you, be gentle in your conversation.
If they don't welcome you, quietly withdraw. Don't make
a scene. Shrug your shoulders and be on your way."*

MATTHEW 10:12–15 MSG

Have you ever approached someone with kindness and compassion in your tone, and her response was anything but? It's hard, isn't it? If you're a softie, you probably replay the conversation in your mind, over and over, wondering what you could've said or done differently. You agonize over the misunderstanding. You pour out your heart to God. "Why doesn't she get me? What am I doing wrong?"

It's even tougher when people completely dismiss you or push you aside. Their dismissal can leave you shaken. They don't care to connect with you. . .at all. Ouch!

Jesus knew His followers weren't intended to be BFFs with everyone. No doubt that's why He added the line, "Shrug your shoulders and be on your way."

Jesus wants you to do your best to live at peace with everyone, but when you're not swept into the clique, don't fret. Brush the dust from your feet (and the cares from your heart) and move on. Without guilt. Without remorse. Without a second thought about what you could've done differently.

Lord, heal my heart from any
broken places, I pray. Amen.

Your Hiding Place

*Let everyone who is faithful pray to You at a time that
You may be found. When great floodwaters come, they
will not reach him. You are my hiding place; You protect
me from trouble. . . . I will instruct you and show you the
way to go; with My eye on you, I will give counsel.*

PSALM 32:6–8 HCSB

There are times when God calls His people to seek Him. He stirs
something within their hearts, reaching past their pain, and
touches their spirits. He wants them to respond to Him. To pray
to Him. For He is eager to answer, to help, to heal.

Throughout His Word, God makes it clear that all He wants
is the best for us. Yet all too often, we begin believing *we* know
what's best. So we step out in the direction that seems to be eas-
iest, safest, most prosperous.

Then, when troubles come, we realize our mistakes and
missteps. We begin to have misgivings, thinking that because
we took our own road, God may not answer us.

No matter where you are, what path you've taken, go to God.
Pray to Him. Let Him know what's happening in your life. Know
that He will hide you, protect you from trouble, and deliver you
for the darkness. Then allow Him to teach you the *right* way to go.

Lord, it's You I trust. Surround me with Your
faithful love as I come to You. Amen.

Forward in Faith

*While He was still speaking, there came some from the
ruler's house, who said [to Jairus], Your daughter has
died. Why bother and distress the Teacher any further?
Overhearing but ignoring what they said, Jesus said
to the ruler of the synagogue, Do not be seized with
alarm and struck with fear; only keep on believing.*

MARK 5:35–36 AMPC

Jairus, a leader of a local synagogue, approached Jesus, then
fell at His feet. He begged Jesus to come lay His hands on his
daughter so that she would live. Jesus began following Jairus to
his house. But soon this mission was interrupted by a woman
with an issue of blood.

While Jesus was dealing with the hemorrhaging woman,
some people came from Jairus' house, telling him, "Your daughter
has died. Why bother and distress the Teacher any further?" But
Jesus had overheard their words. And He ignored them, simply
telling Jairus to not fear but keep on believing. Jairus did. And
his daughter was healed.

Woman of God, Jesus calls you to a life full of trust in Him—
regardless of your current circumstances. He steers you away
from fear and forward in faith. For there your miracle, reward,
and peace await.

There are times, Lord, when fear seems to
overcome my faith. Help me turn that around.
Help me steer away from fear and move forward
in faith. In the name of Jesus, I pray. Amen.

The Light

"We must quickly carry out the tasks assigned
us by the one who sent us.... While I am here
in the world, I am the light of the world."

JOHN 9:4–5 NLT

Walking along with His disciples, Jesus sees a blind man. His followers ask, "Why was this man born blind? Was it because of his own sins or his parents' sins?" (John 9:2 NLT).

Jesus says it's neither. The man made of earth was born blind so others could see the power of God displayed. And Jesus proves His point by spitting on the ground, creating mud with His spittle, and spreading the concoction on the blind man's eyes. After He tells him to rinse his eyes in the pool of Siloam, the obedient man sees a whole new world.

Jesus, the constant Creator and re-Creator, reaches out for what is at hand. He makes a healing salve, providing a remedy that will open new vistas. Trusting Jesus, the blind man readily washes his eyes, and the light of the world comes into his life. And all can now see God's power!

What is Jesus re-creating in your life? What remedy is He bringing to you that's already at hand? Do you trust Him enough to go where He's sending you? What power will God display when you do?

Light of my life, open my eyes to what You are re-creating in my life. Help me trust You and obey. Show me the light.

Power of Faith

"What do you want me to do for you?" Jesus asked
him. The blind man said, "Rabbi, I want to see." "Go,"
said Jesus, "your faith has healed you." Immediately he
received his sight and followed Jesus along the road.

MARK 10:51–52 NIV

Do you remember the 1930s children's book *The Little Engine That Could*? This American folktale, as related by Watty Piper, was meant to teach children optimism and belief in themselves. It's about a little train engine tasked with pulling a long train of stranded freight cars over a steep mountain. Larger engines decline to try, but this little engine takes on the seemingly impossible task. What separates this little guy from the rest? He has faith. He believes. His mantra, "I think I can," resonates throughout his journey.

In the verses above, the blind man was healed by his faith in Jesus, not by medicine, not by treatments, not by specialists. He was healed only because He believed in *God's Son who could* do anything.

Faith in God can help you get through any weighty issue. Nothing is too heavy for God to handle, if you truly believe He can.

Dear God, some days the load seems so heavy, the
burdens so great, the afflictions insurmountable.
Please help me to keep my faith strong, to know that
You will help me with any and all challenges if I simply
trust in You, convinced that You can do anything.

Letting It Go

*Then he said to the crowd, "If any of you wants to be my
follower, you must give up your own way, take up your cross
daily, and follow me. If you try to hang on to your life, you will
lose it. But if you give up your life for my sake, you will save it."*
LUKE 9:23–24 NLT

Have you ever watched a child have to give up something? More
often than not, when she gets the first taste of surrendering
belongings or plans, her doing so comes with a lot of struggling,
complaining, and crying. For no one likes to give up what she is
used to, has worked for, or thinks she deserves.

During His Transfiguration (Luke 9:28–36), Jesus demon-
strated His divinity for three of His disciples. To them He revealed what He had given up to take on human attributes and the
responsibility of healing this broken world. So it's no wonder He
asks His followers to give up their previous lives to follow Him.

Jesus promises so many things to you if you're willing to let
go of what you are used to, have worked for, or think you deserve.
In exchange, He offers you peace, joy, comfort, and a way. Are
you willing to be His follower and gain more than you ever had?

Dear Lord, help me each day to let go
of my life and follow You. Amen.

Hallowing the Sabbath

For in six days the LORD made heaven
and earth, the sea, and all that in them is,
and rested the seventh day: wherefore the LORD
blessed the sabbath day, and hallowed it.

EXODUS 20:11 KJV

God created us to need rest, and He modeled that for us by taking the very first Sabbath. He then commanded the Israelites to follow His example and keep the Sabbath one day a week.

The Israelites had strict instructions about what they could and couldn't do on their holy day. While Jesus' new covenant with believers fulfilled the Law and gave us freedom, modern Christians seem to have thrown the proverbial baby out with the bathwater. Now, we cram our Sabbath day full with sports practices, shopping, and meetings (just like every other day of the week).

However, we can't ignore the Sabbath without consequences. God formed the world, our bodies, and our spirits to have seasons of stillness. Our minds must be still so they can reboot. Our bodies crave rest in order to recharge. And our spirits must worship, so we can experience refilling.

To be fully alive, we need relationships, wonder, silence, peace, and the infilling of the Holy Spirit. All these things benefit from rest. When we learn to truly take the Sabbath, we will call it (as God does) good.

Holy God, thank You for creating the Sabbath.
Help me to honor it and keep it holy.

Preconceptions

Then Naaman and all his attendants went back to the man of God. He stood before him and said, "Now I know that there is no God in all the world except in Israel."

2 KINGS 5:15 NIV

Naaman, commander of the Syrian army, took the advice of his wife's God-fearing servant girl. He headed to Israel to be cured of leprosy by the prophet Elisha. But when that man of God told him to wash in the Jordan seven times, Naaman balked because of his preconceptions of what Elisha's healing process would be: "I thought that he would surely come out to me and stand and call on the name of the LORD his God, wave his hand over the spot and cure me of my leprosy" (2 Kings 5:11 NIV). Fortunately for Naaman, his servants reasoned with him, saying, "My father, if the prophet had told you to do some great thing, would you not have done it? How much more, then, when he tells you, 'Wash and be cleansed'!" (2 Kings 5:13 NIV). Naaman then followed Elisha's remedy and received not only absolute healing but faith in God!

When you're looking to God for answers, trust Him to have the right remedy. Let go of any preconceived notions of what your "cure" should look like. Step out in faith, knowing no matter how out of your realm His notions are, they are what will work for you.

**Help me have more faith in You than
in my own ideas, Lord.**

Turn to God

He turns a desert into pools of water, a parched land into springs of water. And there he lets the hungry dwell, and they establish a city to live in; they sow fields and plant vineyards and get a fruitful yield.

PSALM 107:35–37 ESV

God is always looking out for the common person, the one who doesn't put on airs. His heart is attracted and fixed on the woman who cares about others but may have only one pair of shoes.

For people like His Son, those who have no place to lay their heads nor their own home in which to abide, God turns a desert into a land that will yield fruit. For those who follow His will and way, those who love Him, seek Him, and thirst for His presence, He will provide deep wells of living water.

When you need help, when you feel you are crushed, forsaken, when you have a heart that you feel will never heal, turn to the one who lost His only Son, watched Him beaten, abused, mocked, and then died upon a cross. Go to the one who knows what suffering is. And you will find a well of release and relief, a friend and mentor, an unshakable rock and refuge like no other.

I need You, Lord. Quench my thirst for
love, my craving for kindness. Lift me up,
Lord, into Your arms, until I can stand
firmly on my feet once more. Amen.

He Chose

*The LORD did not set His love upon you, nor choose you,
because ye were more in number than any people; for ye were
the fewest of all people: but because the LORD loved you.*
DEUTERONOMY 7:7–8 KJV

In the book of Deuteronomy God tells the people of Israel that they are unique. Who else has heard "the voice of God speaking out of the midst of the fire" (Deuteronomy 4:33 AMPC) and lived? What other nation could claim that Jehovah was on their side as they saw all the miracles God did for them? However, God says that this special treatment, this unique relationship with the one true God, is not a result of anything done by the Israelites. They did nothing to deserve this love; it was freely given to them. They were actually a terribly rebellious and ungrateful people. However, God still reached down to them and constantly assured them of His love and presence. Women today, and men as well, seek to do things to gain acceptance or affection. They judge their worth by their accomplishments, looks, possessions. But God says He loves His people and it is nothing they do that makes them right with God. It is only God's grace, evidenced most powerfully through the death and resurrection of Jesus, that produces the Maker's love. He chose to love and to save. What's more, He chose to love the least of us.

Father, humble us when we think we can reach You
by our own strength. When we are discouraged and
weary, let us remember that You love us still.

Go. Pray. Seek.

*"If my people who are called by my name humble themselves,
and pray and seek my face and turn from their wicked
ways, then I will hear from heaven and will forgive their
sin and heal their land. Now my eyes will be open and my
ears attentive to the prayer that is made in this place."*

2 CHRONICLES 7:14–15 ESV

When's the last time you humbled yourself before God, bowing, getting down on your knees, or prostrating yourself, realizing who He really is, what He's done in the past, and what He's now doing in your life?

When's the last time you truly prayed, from the heart, not the mind, with no holds barred, putting all the good, bad, and ugly about your world or even yourself before Him?

When's the last time you sought God's face with all your heart, mind, soul, spirit, and body? When's the last time you humbly asked the Lord of lords for forgiveness?

God wants you to know He's waiting to hear from you, ready to see you before Him. Are you ready to be open—totally open—to Him?

Open yourself to God today, in this moment, before your duties take you into that material realm. Know He's as open to you as you are to Him. Remember that you've been chosen by Him, that Jesus has paved the way for you to appear before Him. Go. Pray. Seek. And be continually changed.

To You, Lord, I come, I pray, I seek. . .You.

Deep Roots

*"They will be like a tree planted by the water that sends
out its roots by the stream. It does not fear when heat
comes; its leaves are always green. It has no worries
in a year of drought and never fails to bear fruit."*

JEREMIAH 17:8 NIV

Watering your garden doesn't seem difficult, but did you know
you can train a plant to grow incorrectly, just in the way you water it? By pouring water from the hose for only a few moments
at each plant, the root systems become very shallow. They start
to seek water from the top of the soil, and the roots can easily
be burned in the summer sun. By using a soaker hose, the water
slowly percolates into the ground, and the plants learn to push
their roots deeper into the soil to get water.

Jeremiah talked about a larger plant, a tree. A tree needs deep
roots to keep it anchored in the ground, providing stability. The
roots synthesize water and minerals for nourishment and then
help to store those elements for a later time. Our deep spiritual
roots come from reading God's Word, which provides stability,
nourishment, and refreshment.

Father, I do not want to wither in the sun. Help me
to immerse myself in Your Word. When I do, I strike
my spiritual roots deeper into life-giving soil and
drink from living water. Help me to be the fruitful
follower of You that I am meant to be. Amen.

The Greatest

*"But I tell you, in this you are not right,
for God is greater than any mortal."*

JOB 33:12 NIV

Everyone experiences a bad day every once in a while. You know the kind, a day when you wish you'd never gotten out of bed in the morning. Imagine if that one day turned into another. . .and another. . .and another. . .and each day worse than the last. Ultimately you're brought to your knees and cannot fathom what brought you to this place. That's the well-known story of Job.

Job lost everything. His livelihood, his children, his health. . .and did what most people would do. He tried to figure out why. Three of Job's friends offered suggestions of the cause of his misery, adding fuel to his despondency. It took a young man, Elihu, who finally offered wisdom. Job was trying to use logic of man to rationalize a matter of God. A mere mortal could never understand God's plan. But by keeping the faith, ultimately, a person will be blessed.

Why do bad things happen to good people? We may never understand why this happens. But by keeping the faith, as Job did, God will always bring you through. Remember that next time you have a bad day. If God brings you to it, He'll bring you through it.

Dear God, on my darkest days, help me to remember
that You have everything under control and will
see me through the good and bad times.

Anticipate His Mighty Works

*O LORD, if you heal me, I will be truly healed; if you save
me, I will be truly saved. My praises are for you alone!*
JEREMIAH 17:14 NLT

What tops your list of prayer requests today? What relationship
are you asking God to repair, sickness to remedy, need to meet,
or circumstance to change?

It takes an incredible amount of humility to approach the
throne of the King of heaven and boldly ask for. . .anything. But
the truth is that we don't have to wonder *if* He will act, because
scripture tells us: "This is the confidence we have in approaching
God: that if we ask anything according to his will, he hears us.
And if we know that he hears us—whatever we ask—we know
that we have what we asked of him" (1 John 5:14–15 NIV).

Whatever need is on your heart, your loving Father invites
you to lay it at His feet and know He will meet that need. When
your heart is aligned with His, your desires will be in harmony
with His plans. He will act according to His will—in a mighty,
perfect, and powerful way!

God, I need You to step in and take control of this.
I am struggling, and I need something to change.
If You choose to bring change, I know You will make
something beautiful and whole and perfect. I praise
You for Your good and perfect will for my life.

The Love of God

*May the Lord lead your hearts into a full
understanding and expression of the love of God and
the patient endurance that comes from Christ.*

2 THESSALONIANS 3:5 NLT

God loves you.

Maybe you've known this since you were a tiny child, but despite its simplicity, God's love is so vast—so wonderfully mysterious—that it'll take a lifetime (plus eternity) to understand it fully.

Today, meditate on these truths so you can understand better God's almighty love for you:

- "The LORD is compassionate and merciful, slow to get angry and filled with unfailing love" (Psalm 103:8 NLT).

- "He heals the brokenhearted and bandages their wounds" (Psalm 147:3 NLT).

- "Nothing in all creation will ever be able to separate us from the love of God" (Romans 8:39 NLT).

- "For this is how God loved the world: He gave his one and only Son, so that everyone who believes in him will not perish but have eternal life" (John 3:16 NLT).

- "But God is so rich in mercy, and he loved us so much, that even though we were dead because of our sins, he gave us life when he raised Christ from the dead" (Ephesians 2:4–5 NLT).

There is no better place for you to be and no more secure situation than resting in the love of God.

God, teach me to understand Your love more fully.

The Good Shepherd

This is the kind of life you've been invited into, the kind of life Christ lived. . . . He used his servant body to carry our sins to the Cross so we could be rid of sin, free to live the right way. His wounds became your healing. You were lost sheep. . . . Now you're named and kept for good by the Shepherd of your souls.

1 PETER 2:21, 24–25 MSG

Once you have accepted Christ into your heart, you are invited into a different kind of life—one that follows in the sure steps of the heavenly Father. And this, dear one, is the purpose of your calling.

Because of Christ's sacrifice on the cross, you are free from sin so you can live "the right way." And with Christ as your Savior, you are healed! Not only are you His—He's the actual keeper of your soul! No matter what happens today or in the days to come, if you follow the good shepherd, you can rest assured He will never lead you astray. Following in His footsteps will lead to a life of confidence and joy. Who wouldn't want that kind of life?

Can you imagine anything more freeing than this unshakable life in Christ?

Father, keeper of my soul, thank You for inviting me into a better life—a life where You lead the way for me each and every day. I don't want to do life without You. Amen.

Good News!

"But for you who fear my name, the Sun of Righteousness will rise with healing in his wings. And you will go free, leaping with joy like calves let out to pasture. On the day when I act, you will tread upon the wicked as if they were dust under your feet."

MALACHI 4:2–3 NLT

If it seems like you're constantly bombarded with bad news. . . If you ever find yourself in a difficult place. . . If your faith is faltering and your heart is hopeless. . . If you feel alone and abandoned. . . There's good news for you, dear one!

If you're a faithful follower of Jesus, you're on the receiving end of bountiful blessings. And they're yours for the taking. Part of those blessings include ultimate healing, joy, and freedom in Christ. How can you know this for certain? Because the promises of God's Word are unfaltering and trustworthy. If His Word says it, you can believe it! "God always does what he says, and is gracious in everything he does" (Psalm 145:13 MSG).

Today, thank God for making you one of His own. Praise Him for His saving grace. He is the one and only Redeemer!

Father God, because of Your steadfast love
and grace, I am free. I have joy in my heart—
even when life is hard. You give me hope, not
just today, but for the future. I choose to follow
You all the days of my life. Thank You! Amen.

A Sure Foundation

Therefore, this is what the Sovereign LORD says: "Look!
I am placing a foundation stone in Jerusalem, a firm and
tested stone. It is a precious cornerstone that is safe to
build on. Whoever believes need never be shaken."

ISAIAH 28:16 NLT

When a foundation stone is selected for a building, the largest and best is chosen. It must be straight and solid, able to hold all the weight that will be placed on it. The "foundation stone" that God is referring to in the verse above is Jesus Christ. Jesus is the "precious cornerstone," and He alone is safe to build your life on.

You can trust Jesus to be your home base, the starting point of all your hopes, an unfailing infrastructure. He meets your needs when others fail you. He holds you close when you're afraid. He heals your wounds. He successfully plans your future. He brings peace to chaos.

No matter how tumultuous your circumstances, the promise is that you will not be shaken. What threatens to throw you off balance today? What potential calamity is stealing your confidence? Jesus is bigger than any problem you face. Put your trust in Him alone.

God, I praise You for providing me with the
precious cornerstone of Jesus Christ. Help me
to trust in the sureness of His foundation.

Mondays

*May the God of hope fill you with all joy and peace
as you trust in him, so that you may overflow
with hope by the power of the Holy Spirit.*
ROMANS 15:13 NIV

Ah, Monday! How we love it! (Not!) Most of us dread Mondays because they represent "getting back to work." We live for the weekends, but the Lord doesn't want us to dread our workweek. We need to be excited, hopeful, as each new week approaches. After all, each new day provides an opportunity to love others and share the gospel message.

Think about that for a moment. You are an ambassador of Christ, spreading His love to those you come in contact with. Whether you're headed to the classroom or the workplace, or you're homeschooling your kiddos, Monday can be a fun day, a fresh new start, a chance to pray for God encounters. When you spend time praying for those fun, divine appointments, God always comes through, surprising you with people in your path. . .usually people who need to see the smile on your face or the song in your heart.

So, don't despise Mondays! They are a special gift from your heavenly Father, who happens to believe that every day of the week is pretty awesome. . .because He created them all!

Father, I don't always look forward to Mondays.
Sometimes I dread them. Remind me that each
new week is a fresh chance to share Your love.

Unshakable

Therefore, my dear brothers and sisters, stand firm. Let nothing move you. Always give yourselves fully to the work of the Lord, because you know that your labor in the Lord is not in vain.

1 CORINTHIANS 15:58 NIV

Have you heard the phrase "My future is so bright, I have to wear shades"? The above verse, which closes out the fifteenth chapter of the apostle Paul's first letter to the Corinthians, is reminiscent of that sentiment. Throughout this chapter, Paul speaks of the resurrection of Jesus and the promise of our immortality in heaven with Him forever. Paul reminds us to always serve the Lord and work to His glory. The reward? A future so bright, in eternal life!

Have you ever stood on the edge of the beach, letting the tide sweep over your feet as it goes in and out? Your feet sink slightly into the sand as the water flows by, offering you a firm stance. Think of the moving water as obstacles you face in life. If you stand firm and maintain your balance, you remain steady. You are immovable and unshakable, rooted in the sand of hard work and labor for the Lord. No matter what you face, you will be bolstered by God at all times!

Dear God, encourage me every day as I strive to work hard and labor for Your glory. Help me to serve others each day, to be loyal to You, and to stand firm in faith.

A Deserted Place

In the morning, long before daylight, He got up
and went out to a deserted place, and there He prayed.
And Simon [Peter] and those who were with him followed
Him [pursuing Him eagerly and hunting Him out], and they
found Him and said to Him, Everybody is looking for You.

MARK 1:35–37 AMPC

Jesus, while passing by the Sea of Galilee, had met some men and called them to follow Him. From there He traveled to Capernaum, taught in the local synagogue, and rebuked a spirit from a man attending the service.

Next Jesus went to Simon Peter's house. There He learned Simon's mother-in-law was sick in bed with a fever. Immediately Jesus approached her, took her hand, and raised her up. The fever left and she began to serve her son-in-law's guests. After sunset, droves of townspeople with afflictions, diseases, and demons came to Jesus and He cured them.

The next morning, way before sunrise, Jesus got up, went out alone, found a desolate spot, and began to pray. Yet even there His seeking disciples found Him and called Him out, back into their world.

Woman of the way, even Jesus took a break. Even Jesus knew the only way to be empowered and reenergized was to spend time away and alone with God, in His world.

Lord, here I am. Alone with You once more. May I find
peace and rejuvenation here in Your presence so that
I can continue the work You've called me to do.

Heavenly Guardians

"See, I am sending an angel before you to protect you on your journey and lead you safely to the place I have prepared for you. Pay close attention to him, and obey his instructions."

EXODUS 23:20–21 NLT

Two blind men sitting by the side of the road heard that Jesus was going by. They yelled out to Him to have pity on them. The crowd told them to be quiet, yet the men would not. So Jesus stopped and called them to Him. Then He asked them a very important question: "What do you want me to do for you?" (Matthew 20:32 NLT). Jesus already knew the answer. But He wanted the blind men to voice their exact and definite desire in their own words. Their response, "Lord. . .we want to see!" (Matthew 20:33 NLT), was their way of declaring their faith that Jesus could heal them. Jesus, feeling sorry for them, touched their eyes. Their sight was instantly restored, and they followed Him.

God has sent not just angels but His Son before you, to protect you on your travels, to help you through your transformations, to enhance your vision, to safely lead you where He wants you to go. Pay close attention to Him. Let Him know your desires. Obey His Word. And you too will see.

Lord, I'm following close behind You. Lead me to the place You've already prepared for me. I could ask for no better protective and loving guide as I travel Your way.

Return to Him

This is how the LORD responds: "If you return to me, I will restore you so you can continue to serve me. If you speak good words rather than worthless ones, you will be my spokesman. You must influence them; do not let them influence you!"

JEREMIAH 15:19 NLT

So many of us depend on a GPS to get us where we're going. Back in the olden days, though, we had to rely on paper maps or intuition that sometimes wasn't the best. Perhaps you've been there. . .driving down a road for some time before realizing you're headed in the wrong direction. The only solution? Hit the brakes and turn around. Point your car in the correct direction.

The same is true in your spiritual life. No matter how far off course you've wandered, no matter how many years it's been since you spoke to God, He longs for you to hit the brakes and find the nearest U-turn. He can transform your current situation and make things right again.

So what are you waiting for? Hit those brakes, girl! Don't let another minute go by.

Father, I'll admit there have been times I've wandered far from You. I've deliberately moved in the opposite direction, wanting to live my own life, do my own thing. But I can see now that moving away from You is never the answer. Today I choose to run back into Your arms. Thanks for guiding me home, Lord. Amen.

Choose Happy

A happy heart is good medicine and a cheerful mind works healing, but a broken spirit dries up the bones.
PROVERBS 17:22 AMPC

Feeling gloomy, blue, out of sorts? Do you have an Eeyore personality, always "down in the dumps"? Scripture exhorts us to choose joy, to choose happy. And it's not always an easy task.

When a person is ill, a gloomy spirit can make it difficult for God's healing power to work. William J. Parker, a theologian, stated, "Let the patient experience an inward awareness of [God's] healing force and let him overcome his heaviness of heart and he will find his new outlook to be like medicine." Despite the sickness, we look to our heavenly Father for encouragement and strength, a heavenly tonic. A smile and a glad heart heals us from within and also helps those who come into the circle of its influence.

At times it might seem impossible to cultivate a cheerful outlook on life, but in our Christian walk it should become an intentional act as much as learning to control our temper or be kind. This new spirit within grows from a faith that all things can work together for good when we walk in God's light and look to Him for everything.

Dear Lord, today my spirit is heavy, my heart downtrodden. Help me lift my eyes to You and choose to believe You are at work in my life. Create in me a happy, clean heart, O Lord. Amen.

The Faith Advantage

"If you embrace this kingdom life and don't doubt God, you'll not only do minor feats like I did to the fig tree, but also triumph over huge obstacles. This mountain, for instance, you'll tell, 'Go jump in the lake,' and it will jump. Absolutely everything, ranging from small to large, as you make it a part of your believing prayer, gets included as you lay hold of God."

MATTHEW 21:21–22 MSG

Jesus admitted that in this life you will have problems (John 16:33). Who doesn't? Even those who have money and treasures to fill twenty vacation homes have troubles. But those who are believers have an advantage over all the rest: their faith.

Jesus made sure His followers understood that as long as they had faith, as long as they didn't doubt the strength, the love, and the power of the God who created the universe, the visible and the invisible, they would overcome any obstacles that stood in their way—no matter how huge they appeared!

Some people see their obstacles as something they will never be able to overcome. Their doubts make them stop short, reconsider, then turn and run. They see their obstacles as bigger than their own God!

Yet you're different. You know nothing—no barrier, problem, trouble, or burden—is bigger than your God. You have the faith advantage.

I'm praying my believing prayer, Lord. Help me
triumph over any obstacles that come my way,
for nothing is bigger or more powerful than You!

Up on Your Feet!

There was a man in Lystra who couldn't walk. . . .
He heard Paul talking, and Paul, looking him in the eye,
saw that he was ripe for God's work, ready to believe.
So he said, loud enough for everyone to hear, "Up on
your feet!" The man was up in a flash—jumped up and
walked around as if he'd been walking all his life.
ACTS 14:8–10 MSG

If someone looked at your face during a sermon, regardless of the topic, would he see a woman tired of life, looking at her watch, idly chewing her gum, or drawing a picture on an offering envelope? Or would he see a woman with fire in her eyes, hanging on every word, eating up God's Word, ready for whatever God had in mind for her?

One of the best ways to not get crushed by the worries and woes of this world is to be on fire for God, eager to hear and read His book, faithful to His truths, and excited about *being* the Word, not just reading it.

Woman of the way, dig into God's Word with all your heart, soul, spirit, and mind! Then get up on your feet! Look for where God is working—and head in His direction, knowing He'll give you all you need to further His will and way.

Here I am, Lord! Up on my feet with faith and Your
Word in hand. What would You have me do?

Reconciled

Yet now he has reconciled you to himself through the
death of Christ in his physical body. As a result, he has
brought you into his own presence, and you are holy and
blameless as you stand before him without a single fault.
COLOSSIANS 1:22 NLT

You didn't mean for it to happen. Neither did she. But you and your good friend have had a falling-out. Your disagreement got ugly, and walls went up. Now you're wondering what it's going to take to make things right again.

God is in the reconciliation business. He longs to tear down walls—not just the ones raised between friends, but those invisible walls you've put up to keep Him out too. He wants to restore your relationships, not just put bandages on them. Does that sound impossible? Remember, nothing is impossible with God.

What relationships are you most concerned with today? Instead of stressing out over them, give them to the Lord and ask for His perfect, holy will. Then watch as He moves supernaturally in ways you never dreamed.

Father, I've given up on some of my relationships.
I know there are people I'm not supposed to be
friends with anymore, but there are others who
have grown distant. Today I give those relationships
to You and pray for Your will to be done. Heal and
mend the ones that are meant to be, I pray. Amen.

Nighttime Instruction

I will bless the LORD who guides me; even at night my heart instructs me. I know the LORD is always with me. I will not be shaken, for he is right beside me.

PSALM 16:7–8 NLT

Ah, finally! You're all tucked in, the lights are off, and you're free to just relax. There, in that peaceful, quiet place, the Lord begins to whisper to your heart. He tickles your ear with His still, small voice and gives insight into the problems you're facing. Or perhaps He speaks to you through a dream, giving you ideas about how to handle a situation you're walking through.

Why do you suppose God often speaks in the night like this? You didn't deliberately set out to encounter Him in this way, after all! But, when your mind is finally free from the cares of the day, you're able to hear His voice. You aren't distracted by money worries or relationship squabbles or the roar of the television. You're finally free to just be. And the Lord sees this as the perfect time to give you instructions for the tasks ahead.

"I will not be shaken, for he is right beside me." This is true, you know. . .even when you sleep. So, whatever you're wrestling with during the daylight hours, sleep in peace, knowing God is still on the job, even when your eyes are closed.

Lord, thank You for speaking to me in the night. Even then, my heart instructs me as I hear Your still, small voice. Amen.

A Mustard Seed of Faith

*The kingdom of heaven is like a grain of mustard seed,
which a man took and sowed in his field. Of all the seeds
it is the smallest, but when it has grown it is the largest
of the garden herbs and becomes a tree, so that the birds
of the air come and find shelter in its branches.*

MATTHEW 13:31–32 AMPC

Have you ever planted seeds in the ground? It's awe inspiring to watch that teensy-tiny little seed blossom into a lovely plant. The process is remarkable, if you pause to think about it.

Jesus shared the story about the mustard seed to remind His followers that the burden of proof isn't on them. You don't have to have massive amounts of faith to witness a miracle in your life. You just need a teensy-tiny bit of faith in the one who's capable. If it were up to you (and aren't you glad it's not?), you could never grow your faith to the necessary proportions. But the weight is on God's shoulders, not yours. He's the miracle worker. He's the seed blossomer. He's the one who can take your impossible situation and (with a smidgeon of faith from you) completely turn it around.

What are you facing today? Take your mustard seed and plant it deep; then watch God intervene. He longs to grow your faith as He steps in to take control.

Lord, thank You for growing my faith.
I'll plant my little mustard seed today and
watch You perform on my behalf. Amen.

God Meant It for Good

"As for you, you meant evil against me, but God meant it for good, to bring it about that many people should be kept alive, as they are today."

GENESIS 50:20 ESV

"God can use it for good."

How many times have you heard those words? Maybe some well-meaning person spoke them after you lost your job. Or perhaps you read them in the Bible after the death of your spouse.

There are some situations so intense, so painful, that you doubt God can use them for good in your life. How can He take something so devastating and not only turn it around but bring good from it? It seems impossible when you're badly shaken.

It's time to take inventory. Grab a pen and paper. Begin to list the big crises you faced in your younger years—the things you felt sure you couldn't survive. Now, in a column to the right, list the good that has come out of those once-impossible situations.

There's an old saying that hindsight is twenty-twenty. It's true. Looking back on what the Lord has done, could you conclude that He's truly in the business of turning things around? If so, then He can certainly take what you're walking through now and use it for good in your life. That's a promise!

Lord, Your plan is to bring good from what
I'm going through. So I'll speak words of
faith over my situation, no matter how bleak
things look in the natural realm. Amen.

A Divine Encounter

While he was going on like this, babbling, a light-radiant cloud enveloped them, and sounding from deep in the cloud a voice: "This is my Son, marked by my love, focus of my delight. Listen to him."

MATTHEW 17:5 MSG

Jesus led Peter, James, and John up a high mountain. When they got there, His entire appearance suddenly changed, right in front of them. Sunlight beamed from His glowing face. Even His clothes were lit up!

Soon Moses and Elijah joined Jesus. They entered into a conversation with Him while the disciples looked on.

Then Peter got a (very human) idea. He said, "Master, this is a great moment! What would you think if I built three memorials here on the mountain—one for you, one for Moses, one for Elijah?" (Matthew 17:4 MSG).

Before Jesus could respond, a bright light enveloped them and God spoke: "This is my Son, marked by love, focus of my delight. Listen to him."

Whoa. No doubt you would've fallen on your face. That's what the disciples did. But when they opened their eyes, Moses and Elijah were gone. Only Jesus remained.

Isn't that the way it is? No matter who you want to build a shrine to—even those people you really admire—in the end it's only Jesus who is worthy of your love and praise. Stay focused on Him—unshaken and strong—and He will transform your heart!

Lord, I'll keep my focus on You.
I will give honor to no other! Amen.

Bring It On

So we say with confidence, "The Lord is my helper;
I will not be afraid. What can mere mortals do to me?"
HEBREWS 13:6 NIV

The cares, worries, challenges, and frustrations of dealing with difficult people have an uncanny way of distracting us from the fact that if we're in God's family we've *already* triumphed over every challenge someone can throw at us. We have nothing to fear. We're saved. We are victorious. God wins!

But life happens—twenty-four hours a day, seven days a week. Seasons of discouragement, setbacks, and disappointments shift our focus away from the truth of our situation. People fail us; some may even attack our faith. Instead of looking to the light, we turn around, distracted by the isolating darkness that sets fear in our hearts.

Before these times come (and they come for us all), arm yourself with this mighty reminder from Hebrews 13:6 (a.k.a. Psalm 118:6). Make it your heart's battle cry in the face of every difficult person: "God is my confidence! I will not fear because He is *already* helping me. Do your worst, world, because He is bigger!"

Believe it, sister. He's got your back—now live like it!

Father, I need Your help today. My spirit is beat up
by the constant barrage of challenges from difficult
people. Restore my spirit of power, love, and mental
strength that You have promised me (2 Timothy 1:7).

Headed in the Right Direction

*GOD is fair and just; He corrects the misdirected,
sends them in the right direction.*

PSALM 25:8 MSG

Maybe you've examined a situation you're going through and exclaimed, "It's just not fair!" Why does your child have to be the one with autism? Why is your mother the one with cancer? Why did your husband lose his job when your friends are all living in fancy houses and driving new cars?

Here's a difficult truth: no one ever said life was going to be fair. If it were, then why did Jesus Christ (who never committed a sin) have to die for you, a sinner? That's certainly not fair! But He made the choice to accept the "unfairness," to not let it deter Him. And you can have that same attitude: "I won't give up, even if this is wholly unfair."

Today, look at some of the areas of your life you've been grumbling about. What feels the most unfair? Your finances, aloneness, or health? Acknowledge it before God. Write it down. Then lift that paper up and say, "Jesus, this doesn't seem fair to me, but I won't let that come between us. I will keep on loving, serving, and praising You because I know I can trust You. You will work it all out for good, Lord!"

Yes, Lord! I can trust You! And You will work all
things out for good, even those things that seem
totally unfair. Because of that, I praise You. Amen.

The Possibilities

*"It is easier for a camel to go through the eye of a needle than
for a rich person to enter the Kingdom of God! . . . Humanly
speaking, it is impossible. But with God everything is possible."*
MATTHEW 19:24, 26 NLT

Your God is a doer of the impossible.

At Mount Horeb, God's people were thirsty. So Moses cried
out to God. And God told him to hit the rock with his staff. Moses
did, and water flowed out (Exodus 17:1–6).

When an enemy army came out to fight the Israelites, Moses
stood on the top of a hill. When he lifted "the rod of God" (Exodus
17:9 NKJV) in his hands, the Israelites prevailed. When he lowered
it, the enemy prevailed.

Woman of the way, the Word reminds you that your God
can do anything. No matter what your circumstances, there is
no need for alarm, fright, despair, or hopelessness. For the one
who can part the seas, calm the storms, and make a giant fish
vomit can pull you out of harm's way, lift you from the pit, and
shut the mouths of lions. All you need to do is trust, hope, pray,
and believe. Your God will do the rest.

Thank You, Lord, for giving me the hope and strength I
need to trust in You—the doer of the impossible. Amen.

Encouraging Those around You

Pleasant words are as a honeycomb,
sweet to the mind and healing to the body.
PROVERBS 16:24 AMPC

Are you an encourager? Are your words pleasant and cheerful when you enter a room? Do you find yourself talking mostly about yourself, or do you focus on the other person in the conversation? The tongue is a powerful thing. Words can encourage or discourage, build up or tear down. As you go throughout your day today, seek to be one whose words are healing to the body and sweet to the mind as the writer of Proverbs describes. If you are in the workplace, take time to greet your coworkers with a genuine, "Good morning." Be sure to truly listen for an answer when you use the phrase "How are you?" rather than moving on as if your question were rhetorical. You will find that while kind words encourage the person who receives them, speaking them to others will also bless you. You will feel good knowing that you have lifted someone's spirits or shared in their sorrow. You will begin to focus on others rather than going on and on about your own problems or plans. It has been said that conversation is an art. Hone your conversation skills this week. Speak words of encouragement, words of life that remind others that they're special to you, and more importantly, to God.

Father, help me to speak life today. May my
words be pleasant, sweet, and healing. May my
conversations be pleasing to You. Amen.

The Lightness of Joy

*He gets angry once in a while, but across a lifetime
there is only love. The nights of crying your eyes out
give way to days of laughter.... You changed wild
lament into whirling dance; you ripped off my black
mourning band and decked me with wildflowers.*

PSALM 30:5, 11 MSG

Because you have God in your life, any sorrows you may suffer
are transient, temporary. But the joy you have in God, in Jesus,
in the Spirit, is persistent—eternal. And all you can do is laugh!
For you know that your tears will fade. They will quickly dry up in
the light of the morning. You'll find yourself willingly and easily
praising God for bringing you out of the darkness of troubles and
sorrow and back into the peace and lightness of joy.

How wonderful that after you pray to God, relating all your
worries and woes, He turns things around for you. He changes
your funeral dirge into a song and dance of celebration. He tears
off your black mourning band and showers you with flowers.
Next thing you know you're bursting into songs of thanksgiving
and praise of Him.

If you find yourself in the depths of sorrow and despair, go
to the one who can pull you up out of darkness and into the joy
of the morning light.

Lord, as I pray, take away my sorrows of the night and
lead me with the joy of Your morning light. Amen.

Inherited Blessings

Be like-minded, be sympathetic, love one another,
be compassionate and humble. Do not repay evil
with evil or insult with insult. On the contrary,
repay evil with blessing, because to this you were
called so that you may inherit a blessing.

1 PETER 3:8–9 NIV

In this all-about-me culture, we're encouraged to think about what we "deserve." A bigger house. . . A nicer car. . . A larger balance in our bank account. . . The world tells us that we should have it all. But the truth is, things will never satisfy; they'll only leave us wanting more. God's Word says in 1 John 2:16–17 (MSG): "Practically everything that goes on in the world—wanting your own way, wanting everything for yourself. . .has nothing to do with the Father. It just isolates you from him."

So what truly satisfies and promises unshakable, lasting contentment? God's Word has the best answer: *think of others.* Put others first. Even when it's hard. Even when it's inconvenient. The heavenly Father knows that being sympathetic, loving, compassionate, and humble isn't always easy. But if you say yes to God and embrace this challenge, then you will experience God's blessing—that's a promise!

A life blessed by the heavenly Father is something you don't want to miss!

Heavenly Father, make me more like You each
day. I want to think less of me and more of others.
And I can't do that without Your help. Amen.

The Living God

"I decree that everyone throughout my kingdom should tremble with fear before the God of Daniel. For he is the living God, and he will endure forever. His kingdom will never be destroyed, and his rule will never end. He rescues and saves his people; he performs miraculous signs and wonders in the heavens and on earth. He has rescued Daniel from the power of the lions."

DANIEL 6:26–27 NLT

King Darius made a decree that for thirty days, no one in his kingdom could pray to anyone or anything other than himself. But Daniel, who trusted God with his life, decided to keep praying to God just as he always had. When his disobedience was discovered, Daniel was tossed into a den of hungry lions.

Imagine Darius' amazement the next morning when he found Daniel alive and well—without a single scratch from the lions. This unbelievable miracle caused Darius to have a complete change of heart. And so he made a proclamation that everyone in his kingdom should fear Daniel's God—Darius knew there was no power like the power of the living God.

How wonderful that Daniel's God is still our God today. He still rescues. He still saves. He still performs miracles. He is King forever!

Miracle worker, my King, thank You for being the same God today that you have been since the beginning of time. Your unwavering love, Your promise keeping, help to create an unshakable faith in me! Amen.

No Shrinking Violet Here

And now, dear children, remain in fellowship with Christ so that when he returns, you will be full of courage and not shrink back from him in shame. Since we know that Christ is righteous, we also know that all who do what is right are God's children.

1 JOHN 2:28–29 NLT

Have you heard the term *shrinking violet*? It describes a person who's shy or timid. . .even self-conscious. Does this describe you? . . .

If you are deluged with insecurities and could use a heavenly boost of courage, sister, reread the scripture above from 1 John. This passage holds the secret for standing tall and confident as you await the day of Your heavenly Father's return. The secret is abiding in Christ. Abiding in Him means that you maintain a strong connection with Him, you depend on Him. . .you fully rest your soul in Him, trusting in His promises! Now doesn't that sound like a beautiful way to live?

Daughter of God, you have no reason to be a shrinking violet when you're a child of the one and only King! Ask Him to walk alongside you every step of your journey. He won't let you down!

Father God, I come to You today with an insecure heart. Help me to see that You are with me in every moment and that I have no reason to be timid or self-conscious when I have You in my life. Amen.

So That You May Know. . .

I write these things to you who believe in the name of the Son of God so that you may know that you have eternal life. This is the confidence we have in approaching God: that if we ask anything according to his will, he hears us. And if we know that he hears us—whatever we ask—we know that we have what we asked of him.

1 JOHN 5:13–15 NIV

When you know Jesus. . .when You've trusted Him as leader of your life, you gain a fantastic gift—the gift of confident assurance. As a child of God, you can trust and truly "know" that—

- You are forgiven.

- You have eternal life.

- You can have freedom from fear and anxiety.

- God hears your prayers.

- When you pray according to God's will, He will give you what you've asked of Him.

- And so much more!

Every day of your life, you can trust in His precious promises. What makes this beautiful assurance even better? It comes with an abundance of joy!

What about you, friend? Are you living joyfully through Jesus? Have you fully trusted in the saving power of Jesus today?

Heavenly Father, thank You for the confident assurance
I have because of Your precious promises.

Safe in God's Love

But you, dear friends, must build each other up in your most holy faith, pray in the power of the Holy Spirit, and await the mercy of our Lord Jesus Christ, who will bring you eternal life. In this way, you will keep yourselves safe in God's love.

JUDE 20–21 NLT

Take a good look around, and you'll see that it's undeniable: the world is full of deception and rebellion against God. It's overflowing with false teachings and ungodly temptations. So what's a woman to do to safeguard her heart and mind?

To keep from falling prey to the ways of the world, it's never been more important to remember the simple truths of God's Word. So each day make the choice to. . .

- Soak up the God-breathed scriptures.

- Encourage your brothers and sisters in Christ.

- Pray according to God's will.

- Seek to do only those things that are pleasing to Christ.

- Believe the promises of scripture.

- Take each opportunity to share the light of the Savior.

As you choose to live each day with your focus on Jesus, you'll find yourself safe in His love—and there's truly no better place to be than that!

God, thank You for the unshakable faith foundation that is mine—all because of You! Amen.

The Deep End

I truly believe I will live to see the LORD's goodness. Wait for the
LORD's help. Be strong and brave, and wait for the LORD's help.

PSALM 27:13–14 NCV

A woman is often caught off guard when grief crashes upon her with the loss of a deeply loved one. In those times, she can look to God, her major consolation, her refuge, her true and steady rock. For His Word has an amazing power to reach out, to heal, to catch her heart—and breath.

The words of Psalm 27:13–14 contain such power. They are an amazing balm to help heal a woman's heart torn by loss. For her, they serve as a reminder that good times will one day come again. That God is working in this life, on this earth, among these people. That the pain *will* subside, and then God can begin the healing.

Her part? To not give in to despair. To remain strong and brave. That doesn't mean not shedding a tear, for there will be plenty. But to know, deep down, where deep calls to deep, that she is not alone. That Jesus, sitting right beside her, is also weeping. And that one day, she and her loved one will both rise again. That one day, she will bear a lighter heart and the beginning of a smile.

Thank You, dear God, for comforting me when
the hurt is so deep, and healing me when I am
ready. Help me to memorize these verses so that
I can call upon them in a moment of need.

Always!

"I am the Alpha and the Omega—the beginning and the end," says the Lord God. "I am the one who is, who always was, and who is still to come—the Almighty One."

REVELATION 1:8 NLT

We humans have a tendency to put our hope and trust in the temporary things of this world. We have a laser-like focus on our dreams and plans for the future. And so we spin our wheels and spend our days working so hard to have a perfect family, a lovely home, a rewarding career, and more. We want it *all*!

The "all" should be everything we'd ever want or need. . .right?

Truthfully? The "all" can only be found in *one* perfect being. . .and His name is Jesus. Jesus—who came to save you and me! Jesus—who is the beginning and the end. . .and everything in between! Jesus—who made all things. Jesus—who controls all things. Everything is in His very capable hands.

If you find yourself exhausted and searching for the "all" in this world, give yourself a break. Slow down. Look and listen for the almighty one. He's got a lot to say to your uncertain heart. Let Him fill it up with His assuring love and promises today.

Jesus, thank You. You are the only steady, reliable thing in this world. Help me to depend on You— and You alone!—for all my days. I look forward to a forever life in heaven with You. Amen.

His Will. . .to the End

*"To the one who is victorious and does my will to the end,
I will give authority over the nations—that one 'will rule
them with an iron scepter and will dash them to pieces like
pottery'—just as I have received authority from my Father.
I will also give that one the morning star. Whoever has
ears, let them hear what the Spirit says to the churches."*

REVELATION 2:26–29 NIV

What happens once you receive Christ as leader of your life? If your answer is "I become a changed person," you're right! Once we accept Jesus as leader of our lives, it's true. . .we are changed humans. However, this transformation doesn't happen overnight.

A true transformation takes time and persistence. We should persevere in our faith, so that over time, we grow closer to Jesus every single day. And as we grow closer to Him, our thoughts, attitudes, and actions begin to change. But we can't grow and change all on our own. . .not without Jesus' help! He is our example and guide for a faith-filled life. Following in His steps will help us to change from the inside out.

How have you transformed since meeting Jesus? Thank Him today!

Heavenly Father, I commit today and the
rest of my days to You. I want to live in Your
will and Your way. I long for a steadfast
faith foundation and a transformed heart.
Make me more like You, Lord! Amen.

Creator God

What's your favorite part of God's creation?

- A fiery summer sunset?
- A sparkling blue-green ocean?
- A glistening snowflake?
- A multicolored carpet of wildflowers?

Whatever you delight in, know that the Creator God is worthy of your praise for His incomparable artistry and creativity. Without Him, *nothing* would exist. In fact, everything is dependent on Him—including you and me! And the God who created all things also sustains all things.

Can you think of anything better? What worries and concerns do you need to carry if God is in control? If all of creation is entirely up to Him, what do you need to stress and fret about?

Not one single thing! You don't need to have a care in the world when you have complete faith and understanding that God's got it all—the entire world and everything in it—in His very capable hands.

So let go of your worries today, and give the Lord glory and honor for His beautiful and wonderful creation.

Creator God, although I sometimes take Your creation for granted, I know You are worthy of my daily praise. Thank You, Father.

God Delights in Repentance

"Those whom I love, I reprove and discipline, so be
zealous and repent. Behold, I stand at the door and
knock. If anyone hears my voice and opens the door,
I will come in to him and eat with him, and he with me."

REVELATION 3:19–20 ESV

The Laodicean church is famous for being "lukewarm"—neither on fire for God or totally cold. But what follows its rebuke is today's verse: Jesus' promise that those He loves, He disciplines—He provides opportunity for repentance so that fellowship with Him can be restored.

Amos contains the same promise. The Israelites had committed "mighty sins": they afflicted the just, took bribes, and sent the needy away (Amos 5:12 NKJV). Tired of Israel's empty religious festivals, God wanted to see justice "roll down like waters, and righteousness like an ever-flowing stream" (Amos 5:24 ESV). But despite the Israelites' sins and the discipline He'd already sent, God would heal them if they turned back to Him.

It's the same with us: we cannot go so far away from God that He will not hear our cry for forgiveness, our sincere return to Him and His ways. God keeps seeking us—knocking at the door of our hearts—and if we respond to His call, He will fellowship with us anew.

Jesus, are You knocking on my heart today?
What doors have I kept shut from You? Encourage
me to open them and turn back to You.

Even If. . .

Though the fig tree does not bud and there are no grapes on the vines, though the olive crop fails and the fields produce no food, though there are no sheep in the pen and no cattle in the stalls, yet I will rejoice in the LORD, I will be joyful in God my Savior.

HABAKKUK 3:17–18 NIV

The fig tree mentioned in today's scripture produced fruit that was a food staple in ancient times. Grapes were picked from the vine and used to make wine. Sheep and cattle provided meat. With these things in scarce supply, it would have made sense if Habakkuk had written, "and so I will be unhappy." Rejoicing just doesn't make sense in this situation, does it?

What about you? Have you ever suffered a momentous loss? Have you invested time and labor into something important to you, only to have it all fall apart? Have you experienced a tremendous disappointment? How did you react to life's let-downs? Were you joyful? Or did you spiral into a dark, emotional abyss. . .angry, sad, hopeless?

God's Word says, "Rejoice always, pray continually, give thanks in all circumstances; for this is God's will for you in Christ Jesus" (1 Thessalonians 5:16–18 NIV). No matter what life brings your way—good or bad—*rejoice*! Because you have Jesus!

Father, some days are just hard. It's comforting
to know that because of You, I can have
joy despite my circumstances. Amen.

Ask in Faith

But when you ask God, you must believe and
not doubt. Anyone who doubts is like a wave in
the sea, blown up and down by the wind.
JAMES 1:6 NCV

What does it mean to ask God for something *in faith*? Does it mean we believe that He *can* grant our requests? That He *will* grant our requests? Exactly what is required to prove our faith?

These are difficult questions. Many who have prayed for healed bodies and healed relationships have received exactly that, this side of heaven. Others who have prayed for the same things, believing only God could bring healing, haven't received the answers they wanted.

There is no secret ingredient that makes all our longings come to fruition. The secret ingredient, if there is one, is faith that God is who He says He is. It's faith that God is good and will use our circumstances to bring about His purpose and high calling in our lives and in the world.

When we don't get the answers we want from God, it's okay to feel disappointed. He understands. But we must never doubt His goodness or His motives. We must stand firm in our belief that God's love for us will never change.

Dear Father, I know that You are good and that You love me. I know Your love for me will never change, even when my circumstances are hard. Help me cling to Your love, even when You don't give the answers I want. Amen.

Songs of Praise

*"Great and marvelous are your works, O Lord God,
the Almighty. Just and true are your ways, O King of the
nations. Who will not fear you, Lord, and glorify your name?
For you alone are holy. All nations will come and worship
before you, for your righteous deeds have been revealed."*

REVELATION 15:3–4 NLT

Where is your focus? Are you distracted daily by your own thoughts—does your brain swirl with uncontrolled worries, cares, and stresses? Is your glass half-empty today, friend? If so, give your spirit a much-needed holy pause.

Refocus your thoughts on your heavenly Father—the one who makes all things possible (Matthew 19:26). When you turn your thoughts on Him—and not yourself—you'll be amazed at the transformation of your mindset. Just try it. . .and see what happens.

Repeat today's song of thanksgiving and praise from the book of Revelation.

The words of wonder and admiration will turn your heart to praise. Every sentence is an intentional focus on God—and His mighty works! This song is a joyful celebration of His infinite power and wisdom—and His righteousness!

Aren't you blessed to know the one and only miracle worker, truth teller, and promise keeper? You are blessed indeed!

Promise keeper, I am so blessed to have a
growing relationship with You. Please refocus
my thoughts. I want to think less of myself and
more of You every day. I praise You! Amen.

Unchanging, Constant

"I am God—yes, I Am. I haven't changed."
MALACHI 3:6–7 MSG

In our human relationships, it's virtually impossible to find a person who will never let us down. . .someone who follows through on every single promise. . .someone who always shows up. . .someone who loves us on our good days and our "difficult-to-love" days. No human being is perfect—including us. And imperfect people make for imperfect relationships.

In a world of all this imperfection, what a relief to know that we can have a beautifully secure relationship with the Father! He is steadfast and true to His Word. We never need to wonder where He stands or how He feels about us, because He is unchanging.

When you're feeling unsure, wrap your soul in these comforting scriptures:

- Hebrews 13:8
- James 1:17
- Numbers 23:19
- Isaiah 40:8
- Psalm 119:89
- Psalm 33:11

Praise the unchangeable God! His mercies are everlasting!

Great is Your faithfulness, Lord. And I am forever grateful that I can know You—and that Your love and expectations for me never change. Your constant presence and unconditional love are sources of peace, comfort, and joy. Amen.

Rooted

Let your roots grow down into him, and let your lives be built on him. Then your faith will grow strong in the truth you were taught, and you will overflow with thankfulness.
COLOSSIANS 2:7 NLT

There are few attributes more admirable in another person than a strong faith. Faith-filled individuals appear to have an inner strength that can stand in the face of any trial. They have a faith that seems to grow stronger even as their world crumbles around them.

How can this be? Their faith is rooted in Christ.

In Colossians 2, Paul uses a word picture that describes Christians as trees. These plants take nutrients from the soil through their roots, just as we take our life-giving strength from Christ. The more and longer we draw our strength from Him, the stronger our faith will grow and thrive.

How do we grow a stronger faith that's deeply rooted in Jesus?

- Read and study the Word of God (Romans 10:17).

- Pray (Hebrews 4:14–16).

- Do life with other people of faith (Proverbs 13:10).

- Trust God—especially in the difficulties (2 Corinthians 1:9).

- Thank and praise Him (Hebrews 13:15–16).

Father, grow my roots deep into the foundation of Your Son. Help me to be an example to others of Your true, steadfast, unshakable nature. Amen.

A Generous and Gracious Lord

Oh, how generous and gracious our Lord was! He filled
me with the faith and love that come from Christ Jesus.
1 TIMOTHY 1:14 NLT

In his letter to Timothy, the apostle Paul reminds us of his storied past. Before his encounter with Jesus in Acts 9, Paul was raised to be a zealous Pharisee like his father (Acts 23:6). His Jewish heritage, discipline, and passion were unmatched (Philippians 3:4–6). He hated and actively persecuted Christians. He had active roles in their death and imprisonment (Acts 8:1).

Yet because of God's love and compassion, Paul was forgiven much, and he knew his story was a beautiful example of the saving grace of the Father—of the transforming power of God's love. If God saved this man with such a wicked heart full of evil *and* God trusted Paul to be a messenger of Christ, then God can do the same for you too.

Today, let go of the guilt of your past. God is ready and willing to forgive and accept you. God forgave Paul and used Paul mightily for His kingdom. God can and will use you mightily too!

Father God, today I'm releasing the shame of my past.
I'm lifting my eyes to You and asking for forgiveness and
freedom from the guilt I've felt for so long. Raise me up
and remind me that I'm Your cherished daughter who can
and will be involved in mighty things in Your kingdom.

Contentment

*True godliness with contentment is itself great wealth.
After all, we brought nothing with us when we came into the
world, and we can't take anything with us when we leave it.*
1 TIMOTHY 6:6–7 NLT

As children, we learn the difference between *needs* and *wants*. We need food and clothes and shelter and love. Wants? Well, wants can be anything and often *everything*. Our wants can balloon into an online wish list a mile long, just waiting for the day we click BUY NOW. Because those things will make us feel better, right?

After the initial jolt of dopamine that comes with the thrill of a purchase, we realize *things* don't bring peace or lasting happiness. What brings real peace and joy is contentment. The importance of this spiritual discipline can't be overlooked. For contentment coupled with godliness equals "great wealth." Why? Because when we live in a state of gratitude, trusting that God will supply all we need, we realize just how immensely blessed we are. Paul writes, "Teach those who are rich in this world not to be proud and not to trust in their money, which is so unreliable. Their trust should be in God, who richly gives us all we need for our enjoyment" (1 Timothy 6:17 NLT).

Do you feel anxious, always striving for the next thing, for more? Pause. Rest, relying on God's unending strength and love.

Father, calm my heart and help me to live every day,
grateful for Your surpassing goodness to me.

Heart Cleaning

*Wash me clean from my guilt. Purify me
from my sin. . . . You desire honesty from the
womb, teaching me wisdom even there.*

PSALM 51:2, 6 NLT

After Nathan reveals David's transgression (committing adultery with Bathsheba and all that followed) to him, there's this wrenching plea for forgiveness and expression of repentance. In the first moment, David discloses that it's finally against God that he's sinned. So he asks God to cleanse him; to hide His face from David's sin; to revive David's bones, crushed by his sin, so that he might rejoice and hear joy and gladness. This cleansing will be one with truth that comes in the womb, truth that God desires, and one with the wisdom that God teaches him.

In Psalm 51, David comes to light as a sinner who has faith in a God of unfailing love. So even as he is uncovered as a sinner, he doesn't shrink from making his appeal. He doesn't shrink from the possibility that he can be changed and brought to a better place. However late it may be, David has now become fully aware of his wrongs, and he offers himself with openness and willingness to God, appealing to God's mercy and kindness for forgiveness.

This is the first transformation, the transformation from a proud agent of sin to a humbled and repentant servant of the Lord.

Lord, help me to see my transgressions when they escape
me; help me to cross the road to You for forgiveness.

The Enemy's Tactics

*One day he went into the house to attend
to his duties. . . . She caught him by his
cloak and said, "Come to bed with me!"
But he left his cloak in her hand and ran.*

GENESIS 39:11–12 NIV

The enemy is sly! He comes after you in such tricky ways that you don't always recognize his tactics. That's why it's so important to keep your guard up!

Maybe you've been there. You were trekking along just fine. Then, from out of the blue, you were hit with a false accusation or relationship struggle. You spent the first few minutes reeling, because it didn't make sense. Then, as the dust cleared, you began to see it for what it truly was. . .an attack.

When the enemy comes after you, you can (a) turn and run or (b) look him in the face and call him on his game. But remember, "No weapon forged against you will prevail, and you will refute every tongue that accuses you" (Isaiah 54:17 NIV).

The enemy can try all he likes, but you're God's anointed and covered by Him. Best of all, He'll fight your battles for you. So, don't panic when false accusations come. Don't let the attacks shake you or bring you down. God's going to rush to your defense. All you need to do is quiet your heart and trust Him.

I trust You, Lord, even when everything inside of me is
shaking in anger. I'll look to You, my defender! Amen.

Be Specific

"Be quiet!" the crowd yelled at them. But they only shouted louder, "Lord, Son of David, have mercy on us!" When Jesus heard them, He stopped and called, "What do you want me to do for you?"

MATTHEW 20:31–32 NLT

How those two blind men must have delighted Jesus. They understood what the disciples had failed to grasp.

Jesus had explained that leaders must first be servants, and He pointed to His coming death. The disciples saw themselves in the framework of an earthly kingdom, deserving of honor and deference.

The blind men saw the servant King. "Lord, Son of David, have mercy on us."

Still, their trust fell short. Jesus asked for clarification. "What do you want me to do for you?"

How long did they take to answer? Did they discuss this once-in-a-lifetime opportunity between themselves? Would they ask for a temporary fix of money?

No, they dared to ask for the impossible—for their sight to be restored. Jesus honored their faith. In turn, they followed Him.

Today God invites His children to trust Him in everything, both in general and specifics. He will provide your daily bread. But He also wants you to ask if today's bread needs to include restoring your sight.

Almighty God, I can trust You to do the impossible.

Deep Waters

*He reached down from on high and took hold
of me; he drew me out of deep waters.*

PSALM 18:16 NIV

Have you ever been in a really dark place? Maybe you lost a spouse or a child and drifted into a deep depression, one you couldn't seem to pull yourself out of. Or maybe you were badly hurt by someone you trusted and sank to the depths after the fact.

Life has a way of tugging us downward. And sometimes, in spite of our best efforts, we have a hard time digging our way out. That's why it's so comforting to read today's verse. What we cannot do, God can.

Don't you just love the imagery here? God takes His hand, reaches down, and grabs hold of you when you're in the depths. He doesn't leave you there. He offers a way out. Then (no matter how hard you kick or scream), He "draws" you out.

There's something special about that word *draws*, isn't there? God doesn't yank you out. He doesn't holler and say, "Get out of there!" He gently, lovingly eases you out of the pit and sets your feet on solid ground. And when you're standing on the rock (Jesus), you won't be shaken!

Oh Lord, I'm so grateful for the many times You extended a hand my way. When I couldn't lift myself, You were right there, drawing me out. It's Your name I praise. Amen.

Our Trust Is in Him

Now I know that the Lord saves His anointed; He will answer him from His holy heaven with the saving strength of His right hand. Some trust in and boast of chariots and some of horses, but we will trust in and boast of the name of the Lord our God.

If someone were to ask you, "What do you put your trust in?" how would you respond? Some put their trust in their bank balance. Others put their trust in people. Still others put their trust in the stock market or in their jobs. Some trust in politicians or political parties.

God wants to remind you today that your trust needs to be in Him. If it's in anything earthly (or temporary), you'll be disappointed time and time again. But when you put your trust in the Lord, you will never face disappointment. He will answer you from heaven when you call. (Will your favorite politician do that?) He will reach down with His hand and save you. (Will your boss do that?) He has His grip on your circumstance. (Does your bank account have that?)

No one can do what God can do. No one (or no *thing*) can protect, guard, and secure you as the Lord can. So, shift your focus from the temporary to the eternal. Look to God, your author and salvation. He alone can save you.

Lord, today I choose to place every
situation I'm facing into Your capable hands.
Do what only You can do, Father. Amen.

New Courage

And the [Christian] brethren there, having had news
of us, came as far as the Forum of Appius and the
Three Taverns to meet us. When Paul saw them,
he thanked God and received new courage.

ACTS 28:15 AMPC

The apostle Paul had been arrested, bound in chains, threatened by religious leaders, then put under guard on a ship to Italy where, as a Roman citizen, he would take his appeal to Caesar. Along the way, he was shipwrecked on the island of Malta. There he was bitten by a snake yet lived to heal many of the islanders. After three months, Paul was picked up by another ship and sailed to Italy. It was in Rome where he met up with some fellow Christians. Seeing them, Paul felt his courage renew within him.

When you need a break, when you're disheartened and dispirited, when nothing seems to be going your way, take heart. God will send just what you need at just the right time to give you new courage. To lighten your heart, spirit, and mind. To renew you.

Today, thank God for seeing you through some dire situations. And when He sends others to come alongside you, lift up your heart and voice in praise. His help and their encouragement will make a new woman out of you.

Thank You, Lord, for seeing me through so
many things and for sending brothers and
sisters in Christ to renew my courage.

Needing More

Show me now Your way, that I may know You
[progressively become more deeply and intimately
acquainted with You, perceiving and recognizing
and understanding more strongly and clearly] and that
I may find favor in Your sight.... And the Lord said,
My Presence shall go with you, and I will give you rest.
EXODUS 33:13–14 AMPC

God had said He would send an angel to go before Moses and His people (Exodus 33:2, 12–16). But Moses told God that His sending an angel was not enough. Moses wanted more. And so he asked for more. He asked for God's very presence to go with them. And God obliged.

Perhaps you too feel you need more. You want to know God better, to recognize Him, to understand His ways and means, to find out what He has in store for you and what His plans are.

Many of your questions can be answered by God's Word. Others can be addressed specifically to God in personal prayer.

Yet there is one thing that God wants you to be sure of, to take as fact. Just as with Moses, God's presence *is* walking with You. And He *will* give you all you need along the way—including His rest.

I want to know You more dearly and see You
more clearly, Lord. Reveal Yourself to me.
Walk with me and give me rest. Amen.

Refreshment in Dry Times

"The grass withers and the flowers fall,
but the word of our God endures forever."

ISAIAH 40:8 NIV

The grass was lifeless, crunchy, and brown. The trees had already started to lose their leaves, and it was only August. Flowers wilted, and the ground was nothing but dry dirt. The previous winter was unseasonably warm with very little snow. Spring had been practically nonexistent, and summer was day after day of relentless, scorching heat with very little rain. It was a drought with no change in sight.

Sometimes our lives feel just like the grass—dry and listless. Maybe we're in a season where things seem to stand still, and we've tried everything to change our circumstances for the better to no avail. It is during those times that we need to remember the faithfulness of God and the permanence of His Word. His promises to us are many and true! God will never leave us or forsake us; and He will provide for, love, and protect us. And, just like the drought, eventually our personal dry times will give way to a time of growth, refreshment, and beauty.

Dear Lord, help me to remember Your love during difficult times of dryness. Even though it's sometimes hard to hear Your voice or be patient during hard times, please remind me of Your many promises, and remind me to stand firmly on them. You are everything I need and the refreshment I seek. Praises to my living water! Amen.

Seeking God

I sought the Lord, and he answered me and delivered me from all my fears.... The angel of the Lord encamps around those who fear him.... Those who seek the Lord lack no good thing.... Seek peace and pursue it.... The Lord is near to the brokenhearted and saves the crushed in spirit.

PSALM 34:4, 7, 10, 14, 18 ESV

Anything you need can be found by applying to God. For He is the one listening, the one who will answer your cries and turn your fears into faith. When your courage is faltering, God will *thunk* down a wall of protection, surrounding you, keeping you from harm.

You see, God is looking to meet the eyes of those seeking His. And once that connection is made, there is nothing He will not do to bless you.

Your task is to simply do good things. To look for peace, embrace it. And on those days where your heart breaks, when you feel as if your spirit has been pounded down to the ground, He will be so close to you that You will feel His breath warm your neck. Feeling His presence so close, your spirit will immediately be lifted and embraced by His.

You are my all in all, Lord. As I seek You,
as I turn away from evil, as I look for Your
peace, Lord, be ever so close to me.

Eyes on God

Delight yourself also in the Lord, and He will give
you the desires and secret petitions of your heart.
Commit your way to the Lord [roll and repose each care
of your load on Him]; trust (lean on, rely on, and be
confident) also in Him and He will bring it to pass.

PSALM 37:4–5 AMPC

God doesn't want you to waste your time and energy worrying about the wicked people around you, those who will soon be mowed over. God doesn't want you so focused on the shenanigans of ne'er-do-wells that You miss where He's working and where He's wanting your attention. Instead, He wants your eyes on Him.

Make it a point each day to move your focus away from all things but God. Spend your days and nights leaning on Him, relying on His Word, confident He will bring His promises to pass. Then you will have time and energy to do good, to hang out with the Lord of lords. Then, with your eyes on Him alone, He will fulfill all your desires.

In this moment, commit your way to God. Give Him every little and large concern that's on your mind. Trust Him to work things out. And you'll find yourself walking in and led by His warm, glowing, protective light.

I come before You, Lord, leaving all my cares at Your feet, trusting You to work all things out. In this moment I commit to focusing on and delighting in You. Amen.

An Autumn Hymn

Let everything that breathes sing praises to the Lord!
PSALM 150:6 NLT

Let the colors of the trees reflect the variety of His blessings. Let the crisp, fresh air remind you of the life He breathes into your lungs. Let the birds that greet the sun give thanks for the new day. Let the fox that slips through the shadows of the night bow in submission to the Lord of all creation. Let the wings of the geese that migrate beat out the rhythm of His provision. Let the deer freeze in poses of graceful beauty, revealing the thoughtful details of His design. Let the flowers that close their petals to the cold and the fronds that curl in the dew show you the intricate miracles He works around you every day.

Let the school buses full of laughing, howling children speak of the glories of innocence and renewal and joy. Let the parents waiting at the bus stops remind you of His ever-watchful, tender care. Let the drivers of all the cars in all the lines of traffic tell of the numbers of souls He came to save. Let the congregations that sit, stand, or dance rejoice in the ever-increasing majesty of your Maker.

Let people sing and talk and shout and laugh and pray and cry and hug and hold and bow down. Let every breath be a song of praise. Let every life breathe it out every day.

Lord, You're so beautiful; I praise You and You only. Amen.

"Nothing to Fear Here"

The guards at the tomb were scared to death.
They were so frightened, they couldn't move. The angel
spoke to the women: "There is nothing to fear here."
MATTHEW 28:4–5 MSG

The morning after Jesus' death on the cross, two women—
Mary Magdalene and the other Mary—headed to Jesus' tomb to
keep vigil there. Suddenly, as the earth shook, an angel of God
descended from heaven. He rolled the rock away from the tomb
entrance then sat there on top of the boulder. The men guarding
the tomb were so afraid they froze.

The angel began speaking to the women, saying, "Don't be
afraid. Don't be alarmed. All is well. I know you're looking for
Jesus. He's not here but was raised, just as He said He would be."

Once he'd calmed down the Marys, the angel told them to tell
the other believers that Jesus was alive and would meet up with
them in Galilee. So the women ran off, filled with joy. When they
met Jesus along the way, He too told them not to be afraid but to
go and tell the others to meet Him in Galilee.

The message Jesus gave the Marys is the same message He
gives you. Don't allow anything to shake you up. Don't fear anything or anyone. Simply do as Jesus has told you to do, with joy
in every step.

Lord Jesus, help me to look for You in all things,
to stay calm, and go Your way in joy. Amen.

Great Patience and Faith

*I waited patiently for the LORD; he inclined to me and heard
my cry. He drew me up from the pit of destruction, out of the
miry bog, and set my feet upon a rock, making my steps secure.
He put a new song in my mouth, a song of praise to our God.*

PSALM 40:1–3 ESV

God is always there to help you—even on those days when you're
lower than low, when it takes all your strength to cry out to God.
But there's some effort needed on your part to make this arrange-
ment with God work.

When you need help, you may need to wait for God to move.
And you must do so with great patience and faith. Patience to
not give up but to persistently seek God's help. And faith that
God has heard your cry and will move, according to His timing.

Know that God *will* pluck you from the miry bog in which
your feet are stuck. Be certain He *will* plant you down upon a
rock, making sure you've got your balance back. And remain
confident that when you've had a chance to catch your breath,
God *will* put a new song of praise in your mouth, a heavenly tune
filled with love and thanksgiving.

I'm keeping my eyes focused on You as I wait upon
You, Lord. For I'm certain You'll see and hear my cries
and lift me out of the pit and up to You. Amen.

Respite

The LORD said to Moses, "Speak to the Israelites and say to them: 'These are my appointed festivals, the appointed festivals of the LORD, which you are to proclaim as sacred assemblies. There are six days when you may work, but the seventh day is a day of sabbath rest, a day of sacred assembly. You are not to do any work; wherever you live, it is a sabbath to the LORD.'"

LEVITICUS 23:1–3 NIV

Through Moses, the Lord gave His people a solid foundation on which they can live a balanced life. This structure permits you six days in which to work, but declares that on the seventh day, you should rest, for your well-being. It is a respite from everyday life and gives you a chance to slow things down from earthly activity.

In this fast-paced world, it is important to take some time for yourself and to give thanks to God for His many blessings. How wonderful that you can hit PAUSE on the remote control of your life and enjoy some quiet time with Him. Through God's grace, you have the foundation for a well-lived, balanced life. Empowered through God's perfect structure, you can be the best you can be.

Dear Lord, help me structure my life based
on your unshakable foundation created
just for me. Thank You for considering my
every need, both spiritual and physical,
and for this day of rest. Amen.

Shine on Us

"The LORD bless you and keep you; the LORD make His face shine upon you, and be gracious to you; the LORD lift up His countenance upon you, and give you peace."

NUMBERS 6:24–26 NKJV

Amid people waving palm branches, Jesus entered Jerusalem on a donkey's colt. Perhaps the celebrants crying, "Hosanna" ("Save us!") in the streets remembered Aaron's blessing and thought, *Today God's face shines upon us at last, after so long.* They hoped against hope that Jesus would be the one to restore peace to David's kingdom.

They were right about God's blessing arriving, but it would not come in the way they expected. Humble and lowly, God the Son would lift up His *human* countenance upon them, face-to-face, to be gracious to them and give them peace. Through laying down His perfect life, Jesus would usher in something more precious than kingdoms and land: a no-holds-barred relationship with the Father, a God who is strong to answer His children when we pray (Mark 11:24).

Daughter of God, Christ still blesses you and keeps you; He looks on you with radiant love and grants you daily grace after grace. When all looks dark, turn your face to the Savior's. Let Him illuminate your heart with lasting peace.

Jesus, light of the world, I'm so thankful for Your saving grace. I want to reflect Your light to everyone in my words and actions. I trust You for the strength to do that.

A Change—for Good

*Blessed. . .is he who considers the weak and the
poor; the Lord will deliver him in the time of evil and
trouble. . . . The Lord will sustain, refresh, and strengthen
him on his bed of languishing; all his bed You [O Lord]
will turn, change, and transform in his illness.*

PSALM 41:1, 3 AMPC

God wants to change you up. To have you live a life of love, look-ing out for the weak and the helpless, the poor. To give someone a helping hand. To love as He loves. When you do, when you're there for others, God will be there for you. But even more than that—He'll "sustain, refresh, and strengthen" you when you need it most. In return, when you're languishing, too tired to even lift your head, spirit, and heart, He'll "turn, change, and transform" you!

God looks out for His daughters, the ones who're moving in the world, stepping out in faith and love, being His Son's hands and feet. He protects, blesses, and delivers them (Psalm 41:2).

As you use your love to transform the lives of others, the ones who need it most, God uses His love to transform you, just when you need it most. Whose life can you transform today—for good, for God?

Lord, I am amazed at what Your love can do! Show me
who You'd like me to reach today—for good, for You!

Your Heart's Desire

*Trust in the LORD and do good. Then you will live safely
in the land and prosper. Take delight in the LORD, and
he will give you your heart's desires. Commit everything
you do to the LORD. Trust him, and he will help you.*

PSALM 37:3–5 NLT

It's easy to look at this verse and think, *Hey, if I just delight in the
Lord, He'll give me everything I want!* But when we really start to
delight in the Lord, God changes our hearts so completely that
all we ever want is what *He* wants. When you commit everything
you do to the Lord, you will begin to see how your desires line up
with God's desires.

What does this look like in everyday life? Start your morning
with thankfulness. Ask God to bless your day and to provide op-
portunities to be a blessing to those you encounter. Interact with
God about each issue and problem you face. Thank Him for big
and little blessings that come your way. Seek His will and guidance when you make plans. Pray for loved ones who don't know
Christ. Intercede for friends and neighbors who need divine help.
Be on the lookout for new ways to delight yourself in the Lord.

Lord, I commit my whole heart to You—
and all my plans and ideas. I want Your will
in my life. Thank You for Your blessings and
Your great love for me. Show me how to
delight in You, Lord. I love You. Amen.

Fearless

*"If you follow my decrees and are careful to obey
my commands...I will grant peace in the land, and
you will lie down and no one will make you afraid.
I will remove wild beasts from the land, and the
sword will not pass through your country."*

LEVITICUS 26:3, 6 NIV

Did you ever wake up in the middle of the night, filled with fear
for an unknown reason? Perhaps you had a nightmare. Maybe
you heard a noise. Whatever the reason, the fear was real in the
darkness of night.

In Leviticus 26, God reminds you that He will keep you safe
and will grant you peace in exchange for your faithfulness to Him
and your observance of His commandments. In verse 2, He states,
"I am the LORD." What a wonderful assurance of His sovereignty
and His ability to protect you!

With God's assurance, you can lie down and trust that you
will have peace and protection from all fears. Believe. Have faith
in God. It is such a small ask on your part for security and tran-
quility in your life!

Dear Lord, help me to adhere to Your observances
and commandments. Help me to do what is
right in Your eyes, and to be able to enjoy Your
peace and your assurance so that I will be
unafraid. Help me to face each day in peace.

Impossible Is Possible

The disciples were even more amazed, and said to each other, "Who then can be saved?" Jesus looked at them and said, "With man this is impossible, but not with God; all things are possible with God."

MARK 10:26–27 NIV

This passage from Mark is one of the most uplifting and powerful messages in the scriptures. It is a reassurance from Jesus that with His Father in your corner, nothing is impossible. These simple words pack a powerful punch. What is there to worry about if God is there for you to make all things possible?

In the struggles of everyday life, it's easy to get overwhelmed. But if you carry this idea—that with God *all* things are possible—within you and trust in God with all your heart, He will get you through even the toughest of times.

Sometimes, when you are in the bleakest of situations, it is difficult to see the light at the end of the tunnel. But God *is* that light. He *is* there. When the fog of doubt is lifted, you can see plainly that He's been there to guide you all along. Remember, Jesus didn't say "*some* things are possible," He said "all."

Dear God, help me trust in You completely.
Remind me each day that with You, I can face anything
and everything. For with You, all things are possible.

Impossibly Blessed

"Blessed is she who has believed that the Lord
would fulfill his promises to her!"

LUKE 1:45 NIV

It's one thing to be told something amazing is coming your way. It's quite another thing to actually believe it.

In Luke 1:30–32 (NIV), God sent the angel Gabriel to Mary, telling her she had been chosen to give birth to a son. He said, "Do not be afraid, Mary; you have found favor with God. You will conceive and give birth to a son, and you are to call him Jesus. He will be great and will be called the Son of the Most High."

When Mary asked how this would happen, Gabriel explained the Holy Spirit would come upon her and the power of the Most High God would overshadow her. To this Mary simply said, "I am the Lord's servant. . . . May your word to me be fulfilled" (Luke 1:38 NIV). In other words, Mary believed God's promise. And it was that belief that became a joyous blessing.

Woman of the way, remember that God will *always* fulfill His promises! Take comfort and ease in that knowledge. Then, like Mary, you too can rejoice! You too are blessed by God's promises! No shaking, no doubt, no fear can enter that equation.

Dear God, please bless me as You blessed Mary.
Help me to have faith, to ask that Your Word be fulfilled.
Help me to believe so that I may be impossibly blessed.

With All My Heart

I will give thanks to you, Lord, with all my heart;
I will tell of all your wonderful deeds.

PSALM 9:1 NIV

God, your Creator, is the only one capable of healing your heart and making you whole again. He heals broken hearts and binds up wounds (Psalm 147:3). It's also been said that God can heal your broken heart, but first you must give Him all the pieces.

Have you given God all the pieces? Have you given Him your whole heart? Maybe your heart has been torn in two and you've been betrayed more times than you can count. God won't betray you. He will never leave or forsake you. Maybe you've been hurt so badly you're not sure if God is even there anymore. Ask Him to reveal Himself to you. Psalm 73:26 (NIV) says, "My flesh and my heart may fail, but God is the strength of my heart and my portion forever."

When you build walls to protect your heart, you end up keeping out the bad. . .but you also keep out the good. Allow God to break down the walls of your heart so He can start putting the pieces back together. Then you'll be able to give thanks with all your heart.

God, I want You to have my whole heart. . .all the pieces!
I admit I'm afraid to open myself up to love. Please
break down my walls and reveal Yourself to me. Amen.

Delivery

Deliver me from my enemies, O God; be my fortress
against those who are attacking me.

PSALM 59:1 NIV

The Lord's Prayer is likely the most recognized prayer in the Christian world. And it continues to be learned early in the lives of many people. Jesus used it to teach people how to pray. Part of the Lord's Prayer includes the words, "And lead us not into temptation, but deliver us from the evil one" (Matthew 6:13 NIV). Sound familiar?

In Psalm 59:1, David wrote very similar words when Saul sent men to watch David's house in order to kill him. God heard David's prayer and protected him.

Although David needed deliverance from a physical attacker, enemies can take many forms. Perhaps you're battling illness or experiencing difficult times. Whatever or whoever your enemy might be, raise your voice to God and He will deliver you.

Reciting the Lord's Prayer can bring peace to your mind and calm to your soul. Give it a try. Based on Matthew 6:9–13 and Luke 11:2–4, here's the full prayer:

Our Father, who art in heaven, hallowed be thy
name; thy kingdom come; thy will be done on earth
as it is in heaven. Give us this day our daily bread.
And forgive us our trespasses, as we forgive those who
trespass against us. And lead us not into temptation;
but deliver us from evil. For thine is the kingdom,
the power and the glory, for ever and ever.

Follow Me

*Then Jesus said to Simon, "Don't be afraid; from now
on you will fish for people." So they pulled their boats
up on shore, left everything and followed him.*

LUKE 5:10–11 NIV

Nothing was going right for Simon Peter and his fishing crew.
They had fished all night, trying different locations, but every
time they had let down their nets, they came up empty. They
were at the point of despair. Exhausted, they had basically given
up and headed back to shore.

As they were washing their nets, Jesus came up to the fish-
ermen, directing them to row out a short way and cast their nets
again. This would be like a coworker coming up to you after you
had tried everything you could think of, telling you to try one
more time. Surely, you would be slightly put off, certain you had
exhausted all possibilities.

And yet, something must have told Simon Peter to listen to
this man. So he did as he was told and caught so many fish that his
nets began to rip at the seams! Suddenly the impossible proved
possible. He knew immediately he should leave everything and
follow Jesus.

And so it is with you too. Follow where Jesus directs, and
your despair will morph into delight.

Dear God, I know I can do great things if I follow You.
Please inspire me to rely on Your direction always.

Joyful Promises

Looking at his disciples, he said: "Blessed are you who are poor, for yours is the kingdom of God. Blessed are you who hunger now, for you will be satisfied. Blessed are you who weep now, for you will laugh. Blessed are you when people hate you, when they exclude you and insult you and reject your name as evil, because of the Son of Man."

LUKE 6:20–22 NIV

If ever there were uplifting words to take to heart, it is those above.

Jesus was addressing a large gathering of poor, sick, and otherwise downtrodden people. This crowd was in desperate need of encouragement and help. Notice that Jesus addressed the crowd in the second person, using the word *you* instead of a more impersonal third person of *whoever*. He was speaking to each and every individual in that crowd that day, peppering His words with promises of hope. What a wonderful message to a despondent crowd!

Are you feeling downtrodden or fearful? Read Jesus' words again. The promise of better times is clear. For He follows the verses above with "Rejoice in that day and leap for joy, because great is your reward in heaven" (Luke 6:23 NIV).

Woman of God, rejoice! Leap for joy! God's promises are always fulfilled. Your reward in heaven is guaranteed!

Dear God, thank You! I take heart in knowing
that I am blessed and that my reward awaits me
in Your kingdom! I rejoice and leap for joy!

In the Details

*He also asked, "What else is the Kingdom of God
like? It is like the yeast a woman used in making bread.
Even though she put only a little yeast in three measures
of flour, it permeated every part of the dough."*

LUKE 13:20–21 NLT

Where is God? Where is His majesty, His miracles, the work of His hands in your life?

God is the morning sunrise when it's hidden by dewy fog. He's the oldest evergreen tree in the woods and the budding flower in spring. He's the comforting touch between spouses, the laughter with friends, and the kindness of strangers.

Jesus says the kingdom of God is in everything you see, touch, hear. His kingdom is in everything good. Like the yeast in bread, once it's added, it cannot be taken out or seen and counted, but you can see its effects. The dough rises with help of the yeast, whether it's seen or unseen.

God is like that yeast. He's always working in your life even when you don't see it or feel it. You simply have to trust that His will, His hand, and His way are in the details.

Dear God, I know You are with me. Even when I can't see You. Even when I can't feel you. I trust that You have gone ahead of me and are planning the way and guiding my steps. I trust You, Lord, to know what is best. Amen.

The One

What man of you, if he has a hundred sheep and should lose one of them, does not leave the ninety-nine in the wilderness (desert) and go after the one that is lost until he finds it? And when he has found it, he lays it on his [own] shoulders, rejoicing.

LUKE 15:4–5 AMPC

You may wonder why the shepherd cares so much for just one sheep. After all, he has ninety-nine others for wool or meat. Why should he worry if one goes missing? But the fact of the matter is that the shepherd bought or brought into the world each lamb. He loved and cared for it. The sheep are not just his flock but his companions as he is away from home. Even one means everything to him.

That's how your Lord views you. You were bought with a price and called by name into God's kingdom. Everything changes when you're lost to Him. Everything changes again when you're found by Him.

When you chose to follow Jesus there was rejoicing in heaven. You. You were the one Jesus died and rose again for. You. You are the one He chases after. You. Rest in and receive that Good Shepherd's love, that passion He has for you today.

Dear God, sometimes I forget how much You love me and cherish me. But today I acknowledge everything You've done in my life and what You will continue to do in my future. Amen.

Worthy of Praise

I will praise you with the harp for your faithfulness, my God;
I will sing praise to you with the lyre, Holy One of Israel.

PSALM 71:22 NIV

Easter Sunday is truly the most glorious day of the year for the believer. Just three days after witnessing the death of the Savior, a miracle that defies explanation—Jesus burst forth from the tomb. Resurrection!

Have you ever examined the word *resurrection*? To be resurrected means you're reborn, restored to life. It's a miraculous do-over, a second chance at life, an opportunity to try again.

Jesus was literally restored to life on Easter Sunday, and He offers restoration to us as well. No matter what broken places you might be facing in your life at this very moment, our risen Savior can restore. Broken marriage? He can fix it. Broken heart? He's the best heart surgeon on the planet. Broken relationships? He's the mender of fences.

A God who restores is a God who can be trusted. And because of His great faithfulness, He is worthy to be praised! Lift your voice in grateful chorus! "Lord, You are worthy!"

What a glorious story, Lord! You came bursting forth from the grave, just as You said You would. Your story didn't end in death—for Yourself or for me. Easter is a message of Your faithfulness. I can trust in the one who gave His all for me. Thank You for Your resurrection power, Jesus! Amen.

God Calls You

And the Angel of the Lord appeared to him and said to him,
The Lord is with you, you mighty man of [fearless] courage.

JUDGES 6:12 AMPC

Take a sheet of paper or mentally make a list of how you'd describe yourself. Start off with some physical attributes. Then add personality traits. Once you're finished, consider all the things you listed. Did you use the words *fearless* or *courageous*? Think about how God says He views His daughters. Does your list match His?

In the beginning of Gideon's story, he wasn't a judge or even a hero. But the angel who visited him called him a "mighty man of [fearless] courage." Other translations use the phrases "mighty man of valor" (ESV), "mighty warrior" (NIV), and "mighty hero" (NLT).

When hiding from the Midianites, Gideon couldn't have felt like any of those descriptions. But God spoke of Gideon as He saw him, not as Gideon saw himself. And God knew the plans He had for him.

God does the same with you. He calls you loved. He calls you beautiful. He calls you a woman of fearless courage. Even when you don't feel that way. Allow yourself to be the woman God sees.

Father, thank You for seeing me differently than
I see myself. On the days I don't like myself, remind
me that You love me and created me to do what You've
called me to do. Help me be the woman You see.

The Glory That Awaits

The person whose ears are open to My words [who listens to My message] and believes and trusts in and clings to and relies on Him Who sent Me has (possesses now) eternal life. And he does not come into judgment [does not incur sentence of judgment, will not come under condemnation], but he has already passed over out of death into life.

JOHN 5:24 AMPC

When you were a child, one of the joys of looking forward to Christmas may have been imagining the thrill of owning a new toy. Perhaps you saw a picture of a desired gift or the real thing itself and imagined yourself playing with it for hours on end. Of course, your anticipation may have been more satisfying than the reality. Though you may have loved some of the Christmas gifts received, you may have realized you'd experienced the most joy in going to sleep at night and dreaming of the joy that awaited in those packages around the tree.

Fortunately, we don't have to imagine we'll have the gift of eternal life someday. Jesus tells us His gift of eternal life *is already ours!* Yet we *do* anticipate the complete fulfillment of it.

How wonder filled we can be as we live this life, knowing that now and forever, we will always have God within and with us.

Heavenly Father, thank You for giving me
eternal life through Your Son. I rejoice
in that knowledge today! Amen.

Solid Restoration

When Jesus had lifted up himself, and saw none but the woman, he said unto her, Woman, where are those thine accusers? hath no man condemned thee? She said, No man, Lord. And Jesus said unto her, Neither do I condemn thee: go, and sin no more.

JOHN 8:10–11 KJV

In the well-known story of the woman caught in the act of adultery, Jesus knows very well what she has done—she has sinned egregiously and intentionally. He also knows what the hypocritical Pharisees want Him to do with her—condemn her then stone her.

Instead, Jesus does what no one expects.

He forgives her.

He convicts them.

She is not expecting mercy. The Law is clear on her punishment. But Jesus fulfills the Law because He is soon going to pay the price for her sin. So, He forgives her.

The Pharisees are not expecting to feel convicted of their own sins. But, ironically, the one who can legitimately cast the first stone—the sinless Son of God—reminds them that they're not qualified to carry out an execution based on their own merits.

Jesus was always doing the unexpected. Not because He didn't value norms but because He came to reinvent them—with grace.

Dear Jesus, please give me eyes to see others through Your lens of mercy. Instead of rejecting them, prompt me to point them to the source of forgiveness and restoration. In Your holy name, amen.

What Shall We Say?

*"Now my soul is troubled, and what shall I say?
'Father, save me from this hour'? No, it was for this very
reason I came to this hour. Father, glorify your name!"*

JOHN 12:27–28 NIV

Very soon, Jesus would be betrayed, abandoned, arrested, and crucified. Innocent though He was, He would take the punishment for *all* sin. His soul was troubled, and no wonder! Things couldn't get worse than that.

In our lives, when worse seems headed toward worst, our only prayer may be for rescue. *Get me out of this mess. Spare me from this trouble.* How many of us have the faith to pray, *Father, in this hour, bring glory to Your name*? Yet that's exactly what Jesus modeled. He knew the path ahead would be dark, but it would also lead to glory. So the Savior submitted; the Son put His confidence in the Father's will.

God's ways are not our ways. His *whys*—His reasons—are often not clear. But His providence is beyond question, whether that means we walk through the valley one step at a time or march triumphantly through a parted sea. We can put our troubled souls into His hands because our souls can trust in the one who glorifies His name again and again—and again (John 12:28).

I pray for detours around the difficult parts of
life, but I believe You have a purpose even in the
worst times. So, Father, glorify Your name!

Potter and Clay

"He is the God who made the world and everything in it.... He himself gives life and breath to everything, and he satisfies every need.... He is not far from any one of us. For in him we live and move and exist."

ACTS 17:24–25, 27–28 NLT

God created the world and everything in it—including you. He gave you life and breath. He can, does, and will satisfy your every need. For He is never far from you. Because it is in Him that you live, move, and exist.

Yet that's not the end of the story. For God continues to transform, to re-create you. God, the grand master, the potter, is molding you, the clay, to be more like the woman He desires for you to be, changing your thoughts and attitudes, even your actions and behavior. Making you a vessel through which He can shine His light for the whole world to see.

As a new creation in Christ, God has put His desires in your heart. Your prayers are now more powerful, meaningful, able to affect not just you and others but the world that surrounds you. For He has a plan in mind. And you are a part of that plan.

Father, may You, the potter, mold me, the clay,
into more and more of what You desire.

Songs of Praise

Your love, GOD, is my song, and I'll sing it!
I'm forever telling everyone how faithful you are.
PSALM 89:1 MSG

What is our song when times are tough? What refrain flows from our mouths? If we're focusing on the problems, we tend to harp on the problems, don't we? We tend to complain and lament. It might even seem that we only ever talk about the bad in our world. But what if we changed our tune? What if we sang a song of love instead?

Jesus was an earthly picture of God's love. The apostle John wrote of Jesus, "Before the Passover celebration, Jesus knew that his hour had come to leave this world and return to his Father. He had loved his disciples during his ministry on earth, and now he loved them to the very end" (John 13:1 NLT). Another translation says that Jesus loved His disciples "to the last and to the highest degree" (John 13:1 AMPC)—exactly the way God loves us. Think of it: God loves to the full. His love is never absent and never lessened. We have this love to carry us through any and all circumstances. And that's worth singing about—yes, in any and all circumstances!

Like the psalmist, let's sing of the Lord's love and never stop.

Lord, I feel like a broken record, stuck on what's wrong. Transform my words of woe into songs of praise. Open my mouth to share Your love.

"Lean on Me"

Elisha replied, "Listen to this message from the LORD!
... By this time tomorrow in the markets of Samaria,
six quarts of choice flour will cost only one piece of silver."
2 KINGS 7:1 NLT

The people in Samaria were going through a *terrible* time. The Syrians had besieged the city, which resulted in a famine. Prices skyrocketed: a donkey's head cost eighty pieces of silver; dove's dung cost five pieces of silver. Things were so desperate that mothers were eating children (2 Kings 6:28–29). Good, godly leadership was needed, but Israel's king gave up on God: "All this misery is from the LORD! Why should I wait for the LORD any longer?" (2 Kings 6:33 NLT). And his captain—a man "on whose hand the king leaned" (2 Kings 7:2 ESV)—doubted God despite Elisha's prophecy of relief. "That couldn't happen even if the LORD opened the windows of heaven!" he said (2 Kings 7:2 NLT).

But relief *did* come; God saw to that (2 Kings 7:3–20). Where the leaders lost hope in God, Elisha saw his rock, his rescuer, the God on whom the people could lean and never be let down. In the most terrible times imaginable, God is still God. His promises are still His promises. Lean on that truth today.

Lord, thankfully I have not seen such terrible times.
But in any amount of trouble, Lord, relief is found in You!

Evidence of God and Goodness

"We have come to bring you the Good News that you should. . .turn to the living God, who made heaven and earth, the sea, and everything in them. In the past he permitted all the nations to go their own ways, but he never left them without evidence of himself and his goodness. For instance, he sends you rain and good crops and gives you food and joyful hearts."

ACTS 14:15–17 NLT

When you feel the weight of the world pressing down upon your shoulders, take a break from whatever you're doing and look for the evidence of God that surrounds you. Look for the one who sends believers *and* nonbelievers rain and good crops, food and joyful hearts. See His wonderful creation with the delight of a child—which you are in God's eyes.

Look up to the sky. Revel in the sun, rain, the moon, the stars, fog, mist, light, and night. Step outside and touch a tree. Feel the bark, leaves, nuts, or pine cones. Find a flower. Feel its stem and petals, and thorns if it has any.

Allow yourself to see the world God has made—its wind, waves, rainbows, and people. Permit His joy to enter into your heart, you, another wonder of His own making, a woman of love and light.

Lord, help me to see Your world and wonders
with new eyes so that I may see You and
the evidence of Your goodness. Amen.

At Your Side

"Know the God of your father and serve him with a whole heart and with a willing mind. . . . Be strong and courageous and do it. Do not be afraid and do not be dismayed, for the LORD God, even my God, is with you. He will not leave you or forsake you, until all the work. . .is finished."

1 CHRONICLES 28:9, 20 ESV

Have you ever worried that you won't have enough time or enough provision to accomplish all God has asked you to do?

The young King Solomon may have thought his completing the temple for God was a monumental task. What if he got something wrong? What if God got busy helping someone else on a major project and was no longer around to answer Solomon's questions?

If you know God, you know He'll never desert you until your work is finished for Him. All He really wants from you is to know who He is so intimately that you will never question Him nor worry about what may or may not happen.

So aim to seek God every day. To serve Him with your entire being. Then take from Him the strength, courage, and faith you need, knowing He's always at your side, working not to hinder but to help you.

Thank You, Lord, for giving me what I need to do, what You would have me do. In Jesus' name, amen.

Turned Over to God

*"I'm turning you over to God, our marvelous God
whose gracious Word can make you into what he
wants you to be and give you everything you could
possibly need in this community of holy friends."*

ACTS 20:32 MSG

Some days are harder than others. Some days the obstacles before us seem insurmountable. We are like the newly freed Israelites, with the Red Sea on one side and a magnificent army of warriors with horses and chariots on the other. We think, *There's no way I'm getting out of here unscathed!*

And then we remember whose children we are.

We're children of the God who can divide seas, split rocks, and make the earth shake. We've an all-powerful being on our side who hears our cries, however faint, however pained. We're the daughters of an eternal King of kings who'll never leave or abandon us.

With God in our lives, we can leave our obstacles in His hands, confident He'll remove them. He's the one who has already rescued us from death and loves us like no other ever could.

Today, remember who you are and who God is. Immerse yourself in His Word, put yourself in His hands, and you will become all you were ever made to be and have all you could ever possibly hold.

I put myself into Your hands today, Lord.
Make me what You want me to be and grant me
all I could possibly need. In Jesus' name, amen.

The Hard Times

Not only so, but we also glory in our sufferings,
because we know that suffering produces perseverance;
perseverance, character; and character, hope.

ROMANS 5:3–4 NIV

A blacksmith knows how much heat it takes to create a sword. A jewelry maker knows all the pressure a diamond goes through before it becomes beautiful. A glassblower knows the timing of how long her creation must stay in the fire for it to become exactly how she wants it. God knows the same about you.

The Message says it like this: "There's more to come: We continue to shout our praise even when we're hemmed in with troubles, because we know how troubles can develop passionate patience in us, and how that patience in turn forges the tempered steel of virtue, keeping us alert for whatever God will do next" (Romans 5:3–4).

God doesn't cause your struggles and the hard times, but you can be sure He will use them to help transform you into the precious daughter He created you to be. The hard times were never supposed to be a part of the story, but that's why Jesus came. He's rewritten the story.

God, thank You for taking what's hard in my life
and making it good. I don't know why things happen,
but I do know that You love me deeply and will do
what is best for me. This is what gives me hope, boosts
my faith, and lifts my voice in praise of You. Amen.

The Healing of Discipline

*Lord, your discipline is good, for it leads to life and
health. You restore my health and allow me to live!
Yes, this anguish was good for me, for you have
rescued me from death and forgiven all my sins.*

ISAIAH 38:16–17 NLT

Life is full of good things: friendships, ice cream, sunsets, and
discipline. Yes, discipline! Though it may not seem enjoyable,
discipline from the heart of an affectionate God is good. In fact,
it's better than good because "it leads to life and health." Discipline opens your heart to hear what truth God wants to speak
to you privately.

When you are trained under God's careful supervision, you
live a fuller, more abundant life. Even your mental, emotional, and
physical health are affected positively. Yet know that all suffering
is not discipline, and all discipline isn't for correction. Even Jesus
"learned obedience from what he suffered" (Hebrews 5:8 NIV).

Are you currently experiencing God's discipline? If so, recognize that this temporary pain stretches and broadens you. It
develops your character and capacity to experience the fullness of
joy. You can trust God's training is good, His purpose is to restore
and rescue you, and that He loves you more than you'll ever know.

God, I trust You to work in my life in any way that
you deem best. I'm grateful to be considered Your
daughter and worthy of Your loving attention.

$x = Jesus$

Thank God! The answer is in Jesus Christ our Lord.
ROMANS 7:25 NLT

In chapter 7 of Romans, Paul's words read like a long-winded and complicated word problem in a math textbook. Paul + Law + sin = bad. Paul + Law – sin = good. He continues to say he knows what's right, but his human nature forces him to do wrong. It's an unending cycle of good to bad to redemption to good again and so on. . . . Paul asks helplessly if anyone will save him from this vicious circle of misery and death.

Then the apostle shares the answer he's found. The missing part of every equation Paul posed is Jesus. Jesus can save Paul from the cycle. Jesus + Paul = forgiven and saved. Jesus is the x, the cross that changes everything.

Jesus can be your answer too. He can be the answer to the grasp a sin has on your life. He can be the answer to that unending cycle of heartbreak, loneliness, anger, or sadness. He can encourage you toward the help you may need and the comfort you crave.

All you have to do is start adding Jesus to the equation.

Father, thank You for Jesus and what He's done, saving me from eternity without You. And He now wants to save me from the brokenness of this world. Lord, although I might not get every answer I want on this side of life, I know Jesus is the ultimate solution. Amen!

God Knows You

*The Spirit helps us in our weakness. For we do not know
what to pray for as we ought, but the Spirit himself
intercedes for us with groanings too deep for words.*

ROMANS 8:26 ESV

Your heavenly Father knows your heart. He knows your dreams. And He knows when those dreams are shattered. He empathizes and cries with You. The heartbreak you have to endure was never supposed to be a part of His plan. That's why He sent Jesus to save this world and the Spirit to reside with you in it.

When life is too hard for words, the Spirit is able to speak for you. You don't have to know what to pray. You can just call on the Lord and He'll listen. In a world that seems to be full of talking heads on phones, televisions, and computers, and in crowded stores or restaurants, you can still feel extremely lonely.

Time with God in solitude and silence may not be a quick fix for this feeling of aloneness, but it can be a reminder that God is here with you and for you. And He knows you well enough that you don't even have to speak a word.

God, thank You for knowing me so deeply that
I don't have to explain my pain and hurt to
You. Instead, I'll rest in the silence with You,
garnering Your strength and peace.

Conviction

And Nehemiah continued, "Go and celebrate with
a feast of rich foods and sweet drinks, and share
gifts of food with people who have nothing prepared.
This is a sacred day before our Lord. Don't be dejected
and sad, for the joy of the LORD is your strength!"
NEHEMIAH 8:10 NLT

God's people were sad because they were being convicted of their sin. The Law, God's Word, was doing what it was supposed to. It was revealing how they'd all misstepped in their walk with the Lord.

Sometimes that kind of truth can hurt. And God's people were definitely feeling the guilt and shame associated with their wrongdoing.

But Nehemiah didn't want the people to linger upon this hurt. He knew God was more than willing to rescue them from their sin. He wanted to remind them that the most important part of God's Word isn't that His people are sinners but that God is a Savior.

You can find joy from the Lord in this truth too. Even when you're feeling convicted and sad, you can rejoice in the fact that God is transforming you into the woman you were meant to be. From this joy can come the unshakable strength to move forward in God's will.

God, thank You for correction and compassion.
Even though acknowledging my missteps
is uncomfortable, it brings me closer to
You and Your plans for me. Amen.

Wait for the Morning

I wait for the Lord more than watchmen wait for the morning, more than watchmen wait for the morning.

PSALM 130:6 NIV

Watchmen were guards who stood on the walls of ancient cities to look out for enemies. These men would sound an alarm if they saw danger approaching. This alert allowed the men of the city to prepare to protect their families.

When you were a watchman, it was important to stay awake during the night hours. But this was more than difficult. For the night was dark with no city lights to help you see off into the distance. Torchlight only traveled so far. Not only was it difficult to see, but the hours seemed so long without anything to help pass the time. The watchmen were never sure what might happen in those pitch-black nights.

Many women today may feel like those watchmen of ancient days. Life may seem dark, long, and unpredictable. But just as the watchman waited for the first rays of sunshine to come over the horizon, God's daughters must wait to see their Father working.

The watchmen trusted that morning would come. And it always did. Just as it will for you. For God always works and reveals Himself to His beloved at just the right time.

Lord, when I'm in a dark place, I promise to wait for Your guidance more than watchmen wait for the morning, more than watchmen wait for the morning.

Second Chances

"I, even I, am he who blots out your transgressions,
for my own sake, and remembers your sins no more."
ISAIAH 43:25 NIV

How many of us have hung our heads low, knowing we really messed up? Wishing we could redo that homework assignment, take back the unkind words that leaped from our mouths without thinking, or even pull back that email message right after we clicked SEND. We've all done something we wished we could undo. Often, we think we have failed not only ourselves but also God.

In fact, the Bible is full of people that God used despite their errors. Moses had an anger problem. David was lustful. Jacob was deceptive. The wonderful thing about our faith is that we serve a God of second chances. Not only is He willing, He wants us to confess our sins so He can forgive us. Sing praises for the wonderful blessing of starting over!

Gracious and heavenly Father, we are grateful that we serve a God of second chances. In fact, You give us more than two chances, and You don't keep score. We are all prodigals, and we need to feel Your love and forgiveness. Thank You for loving me enough to not give up on me. You are still with me! Amen.

The Miracle of You

I praise you because I am fearfully and wonderfully made; your works are wonderful, I know that full well.
PSALM 139:14 NIV

Birth is often referred to as a miracle and with good reason. Each child born is so delightfully made, so perfect in God's eyes. Why? Because each child is wonderfully made in His image.

This creation and the Creator are indeed awe inspiring. David, in today's verse, sang God's praises, overwhelmed by the majesty of his existence. God, capable of making such a biological masterpiece, is worthy of being worshipped and admired.

There's no doubt that you too are wonderfully made. Even if you may feel or have been told you are imperfect, there is no reason to be disheartened or discouraged. For God sees all His children as perfect.

Today and every day, give God the praise He deserves, because He made you the incredible, unshakable person you are. Anytime you doubt your significance or relevance, just remember who made you. That unparalleled Creator, He who never makes mistakes and never takes shortcuts. As His creature, you are destined to do great things, because you are God's marvel, uniquely and wonderfully made.

Dear God, I know that by Your hands, I am fearfully and wonderfully made. I stand in awe of Your magnificence! When I feel unworthy or downtrodden, when I'm disheartened or discouraged, help me remember I'm perfect in Your eyes. Amen and amen!

Beautiful Messages

*How beautiful on the mountains are the feet of the
messenger who brings good news, the good news of peace
and salvation, the news that the God of Israel reigns!*

ISAIAH 52:7 NLT

The beauty of God's creation is all around. From the explosion of jewel-toned autumn leaves to the bubbling, infectious giggle of a preschooler, we can see God's joy, peace, and harmony—if we take the time to notice it.

Appreciating God's gifts is good. It anchors us deep in His unending love and reassures us of His presence, protection, and provision. But once we've grasped hold of this truth, it's time to share it with the people around us and fully experience the good news of peace and grace. You are an influencer. Each of us—CEOs of corporations to stay-at-home moms alike—have an impact on our world. Our words and actions affect friends, coworkers, neighbors, and even perfect strangers we encounter each day.

You, lovely sister in Christ, have a beautiful message to share. Tell a friend what God's doing in your life. Talk about God's faithfulness in a difficult situation, how walking with Him made you unshakable. Encourage someone—just because. Ask God to saturate your soul with His love so that it overflows into your thoughts, conversations, and deeds.

Father, thank You for the opportunity to be Your
messenger. Help me to live authentically, with a pure
heart for Your ways. Give me eyes to see others the
way You see them—as Your cherished children.

True Blue

"God is not a man, so he does not lie. He is not human,
so he does not change his mind. Has he ever spoken and
failed to act? Has he ever promised and not carried it
through? . . . God has blessed, and I cannot reverse it!"

NUMBERS 23:19–20 NLT

Balak, the king of Moab, didn't know what he was in for when he asked Balaam (a sort of "prophet for hire") to curse the Israelites. Balak seemed to think that if he made the proper number of sacrifices on the right mountaintop, then Israel's God would be willing to turn against His people. But when Balaam tried to curse Israel, God would only allow him to bless His chosen nation.

The Moabite king found out the truth: God keeps His promises, and absolutely no one can undo His blessings.

Sing of that truth with David, relying in all things on your Savior's care: "My heart is confident in you, O God. . . No wonder I can sing your praises!" (Psalm 57:7 NLT). Trust God's integrity when He calls you to join His work, so you can experience the blessing Elizabeth gave Mary: "You are blessed because you believed that the Lord would do what he said" (Luke 1:45 NLT).

Be confident in your God! His character is firm—He's true blue, through and through.

Father God, as spring renews the earth,
let my heart be renewed by Your blessing today.

Consider All the Things

"But be sure to fear the LORD and serve him faithfully with all your heart; consider what great things he has done for you."

1 SAMUEL 12:24 NIV

God has been your constant companion. Not only did He create you and plan your exact entrance onto the kingdom calendar, He gave you hope and a future. His love has always been there, although sometimes hard to see. But through the ups and downs of life, He's been right next to you, going before you, or carrying you.

Think about the great things God's done in your life. Can you remember the doors He opened for you, as well as all the doors He closed? What about the times money showed up unexpectedly or a bill was paid anonymously? Maybe your health battle was miraculously healed or a prodigal child came home. Have you been able to look back on a tough season of life and see why God allowed the things He did? Was a marriage restored? Did an unexpected friendship develop?

Spend some time this week considering all the wonderful ways God has impacted your life; then thank Him. Let Him know you see His fingerprints on your life. Tell God all the ways He's been an amazing Father to you!

Lord, looking back at all the things You've done for me is humbling. Forgive me for not recognizing and acknowledging Your hand in my life more. I'm going to change that.

Teach Me Your Paths

Show me your ways, LORD, teach me your paths.
Guide me in your truth and teach me, for you are God
my Savior, and my hope is in you all day long.

PSALM 25:4–5 NIV

This psalm is a great prayer to memorize and keep close in your mind each day. The Bible tells us that God's Word is a lamp for our feet (Psalm 119:105). As we read, study, and hide God's Word in our hearts, the Holy Spirit will bring those words to mind to guide us and show us the way that God wants us to go. If you want to hear God's voice and know His will for your life, get into His Word.

Hebrews 4:12 tells us that the scriptures are living and active. Just think about that for a moment. God's Word is alive! As busy women, it can be difficult to find the time to open the Bible and meditate on the message—but it's *necessary* if you want God to teach you His path for your life.

Instead of giving up on finding time for Bible reading, get creative. Download a free Bible application on your phone. Have a daily scripture reading and devotion emailed to you from heartlight.org. Jot down a few verses on a note card to memorize. There are many ways to get in the Word of God and be trained by it. Start today!

Lord, I believe Your Word is living and active. I want
to know Your will for my life. Help me get in Your Word
more and understand Your plan for me. Amen.

Heart Vision

As they were leaving Jericho, a huge crowd followed.
Suddenly they came upon two blind men sitting alongside
the road. When they heard it was Jesus passing, they
cried out, "Master, have mercy on us! Mercy, Son of
David!" The crowd tried to hush them up, but they got
all the louder, crying, "Master, have mercy on us! Mercy,
Son of David!" . . . They said, "Master, we want our eyes
opened. We want to see!" Deeply moved, Jesus touched
their eyes. They had their sight back that very instant.

MATTHEW 20:29–31, 33–34 MSG

In this fascinating account from the Gospel of Matthew, two blind men call out to Jesus—and they're persistent. Repeatedly they say, "Master! . . . Son of David!" They beg Jesus for healing; and, being deeply moved, He obliges.

Jesus performed many miracles during His time on earth, and this particular story of healing might not seem special in comparison, except that it brings to light this fact: the *blind* men "saw" Jesus; while the *seeing* men—like the Pharisees, Sadducees, and scribes—did not. What a contrast between those with faith and those without! The blind men saw with their hearts what their eyes could not!

Dear one, how is your "sight"? If it needs correcting, go to the Lord in prayer. Ask. . .and He will restore your heart vision!

Lord, help me to stretch and grow my faith.
If my heart vision is failing, I trust You to restore it.

A Holy Hallelujah

There was great joy in Jerusalem, for since the days
of Solomon son of David king of Israel there had been
nothing like this in Jerusalem. The priests and the Levites
stood to bless the people, and God heard them, for their
prayer reached heaven, his holy dwelling place.

2 CHRONICLES 30:26–27 NIV

When Hezekiah became king, there was a glorious time of repentance, consecration, worship, sacrifices, praises, healing, and jubilation. This young king was determined to make things right with God. And you could say that there was indeed a real hallelujah time that flowed through the land and the hearts of the Israelites!

Yes, for a time, all was made right. The people's prayers reached heaven. Healing and restoration came down from God's holy dwelling place. The music of cymbals, harps, lyres, trumpets, and singing filled the temple. Rejoicing and happiness reigned.

Today, with Christ's help, may we take a prayerful and heartfelt assessment of our transgressions. May we respond to that divine nudge toward repentance and experience the fresh freedom of forgiveness. May our land be healed and our souls transformed into the likeness of Christ. This dark and hurting world is in great need of a holy hallelujah!

Oh Lord, my Redeemer and friend, together may we
transform this day into a holy hallelujah. Amen.

Everlasting Life and Love

*They sang responsively, praising and giving thanks
to the Lord, saying, For He is good, for His mercy and
loving-kindness endure forever toward Israel.*

EZRA 3:11 AMPC

What a celebration Israel held after beginning the restoration of temple worship. Trumpets sounded, cymbals crashed, voices raised in song.

Most shouted for joy. Some wept, remembering the glory of Solomon's temple, destroyed during the exile of the Israelites.

Solomon's temple had replaced the tabernacle built under Moses' direction. And the offerings God commanded for Moses' tabernacle pointed back to the offerings made by Cain (given out of obligation) and Abel (given out of love), and the difference between them.

God has always weighed the heart of the giver more than the offering. The temple offered hope of forgiveness and redemption, but it was only temporary. A permanent change of heart was needed.

Fast-forward to the final sacrifice, given once for all: Jesus' death on the cross. His blood covers our sin and runs through our hearts, rejuvenating, renewing, giving new life.

"God demonstrates his own love for us in this: While we were still sinners, Christ died for us" (Romans 5:8 NIV).

That's a love story for the ages. That's a reason to celebrate!

Merciful and loving God, I fall at Your feet
in repentance and with joy. Amen.

Old and Gray

*For you have been my hope, Sovereign LORD, my confidence
since my youth. From birth I have relied on you; you brought
me forth from my mother's womb. I will ever praise you.*

PSALM 71:5–6 NIV

Aging. That word doesn't always bring positive thoughts to mind.
After all, each year adds wrinkles and aches. Each year makes the
list of trials we've lived through get longer. Yet growing older is
a blessing also.

The writer of Psalm 71 had experienced hardship, and it
wasn't letting up in his old age. Yet God was still faithful. It was
God whom he depended on the day he was born, and it would be
God whom he depended on to revive him every day of his life. He
wrote of God: "Though you have made me see troubles, many and
bitter, you will restore my life *again*; from the depths of the earth
you will *again* bring me up" (v. 20 NIV, emphasis added). With each
passing year, the psalmist witnessed God's faithfulness firsthand,
over and over, and that boosted his faith. In fact, the good things
God had done were so far beyond number and knowledge that
the psalmist could "hope continually" and praise God "more and
more" despite any trouble (vv. 14–15 ESV).

If you allow it, growing older can increase your faith too.

God, help me grow closer to You as I grow older.
You are faithful, and I will ever praise You! Amen.

God's Light

We use God's mighty weapons, not worldly weapons,
to knock down the strongholds of human reasoning and
to destroy false arguments. We destroy every proud obstacle
that keeps people from knowing God. We capture their
rebellious thoughts and teach them to obey Christ.

2 CORINTHIANS 10:4–5 NLT

Although your thoughts cannot be seen or heard (except by you, of course), they are immensely important. What you believe to be true in your heart comes directly from what you think in your mind. And just because you think a thought doesn't make it the truth. Your mind is always trying to make sense of situations and can land on incorrect assumptions. That's why you must allow God to work in you so you will "be transformed by the renewing of your mind" (Romans 12:2 NIV).

One of God's mighty weapons is to reveal truth where there's a lie. Satan loves for you to believe falsehoods, which can develop quickly into a stronghold of belief.

Ask God to renew your mind and shed light onto any lies you have accepted as truth. Do you believe the lie that you are unloved, inadequate, or unacceptable? Memorize verses that remind you who you are in Christ. Trust God to renew your mind daily in the specific areas that He will reveal. When you do, you will know Him fully and in truth.

God, please transform me by renewing my
mind. I want to know You more fully.

Leave It All at the Cross

As for me, may I never boast about anything except
the cross of our Lord Jesus Christ. Because of that
cross, my interest in this world has been crucified,
and the world's interest in me has also died.

GALATIANS 6:14 NLT

So often we allow the troubles and cares of life to weigh us down. We get depressed or give way to fear. During political seasons we get worked up and allow ourselves to feel despair over the condition of our county, state, or nation.

God wants us to care about the goings-on around us, but they shouldn't be a driving force in our lives. Instead we're to drop our cares in a place where He exchanges our anguish with hope. That place is the cross.

When Jesus died on the cross, He accomplished all that needed to be accomplished. His death, burial, and resurrection didn't just ensure our place in heaven, it gave us a way to live in victory and peace, unencumbered by the troubles each day might bring.

What's holding you back today? Have you left it at the cross? Release it to the Lord and watch Him free you up to live a full, abundant life.

Father, today I come to the cross, not just to lay
my burdens at Your feet but to thank You for being
my burden bearer. How can I ever repay You?
From the bottom of my heart, I bring You praise. Amen.

Scripture Index

OLD TESTAMENT

NEW TESTAMENT